Florence M Scriven

La Donna Velata.

*From the Painting by Raphael in the Pitti Gallery
at Florence.*

The Central Italian Painters

of the

Renaissance

BY

BERNHARD BERENSON

Author of "Venetian Painters of the Renaissance," "Lorenzo
Lotto: An Essay in Constructive Art Criticism," etc.

SEVENTH IMPRESSION

G. P. PUTNAM'S SONS

NEW YORK   LONDON
27 WEST TWENTY-THIRD STREET   24 BEDFORD STREET, STRAND
The Knickerbocker Press
1908

The Knickerbocker Press, New York

CONTENTS.

THE CENTRAL ITALIAN PAINTERS OF THE RENAISSANCE.

The consistent pursuit of the Florentine painters was form and movement; of the Venetians, splendour and harmony of colour: what did the Central Italians contribute to the magic of Renaissance art? Rarely does colour penetrate the senses and warm the heart more quickly than in certain frescoes or panels of Simone Martini or Gentile da Fabriano, of Perugino or Raphael. Yet even these great masters could be at times indifferent, or, indeed, harsh, while their inferiors owe slight merit as colourists. Seldom have problems of form and movement been better solved than by Signorelli; but he had few, if any, followers. It is not with the magicians in colour and the creators in form that the Central Italian Painters, as a school, hold high rank.

What is it, then, that gives them their place not only with the greatest, but with the most popular names in art? Our present quest, if successful, will yield an answer.

I.

Every time we see an object we carry away in our memory some shadow of its shape and colour. This ghost of animate or inanimate things, passing under the name of "visual image," haunts different minds in different degrees. Some people scarcely recognise its presence, although they know it exists; others can at will conjure up shadows so defined that they, in their turn, evoke emotions after their kind, and tinged with the poignancy of the feelings aroused by the objects themselves; still others need only shut their eyes to see absent shapes with the vividness and warmth of direct retinal impressions. Strictly speaking, each person varies from every other in the richness of his visual images, but for our purpose it suffices to distribute all people into the three classes we have just defined. Of the first, we say that they visualise badly, or not at all; of the second, that they visualise fairly; of the third, that they visualise perfectly.

The course of art would probably have been a very different one if people had never visualised at all, or had always visualised perfectly. Had we no faculty whatever for calling up the shapes of things, it might never have given us pleasure to see mere reproductions of them. Why should it? Nor should we be any more likely to care for mere reproductions if we had within ourselves the faculty of calling up at will perfect visual images. But most of us belong to the second class—those who have a moderate power of visualising. When objects are named, some image of them looms up in our minds. It is, however, apt to be so vague, so elusive, that it tantalises rather than satisfies. After a vain effort to fix the image of an absent friend, the crudest manual reproduction may be pounced upon with pleasure, and a photograph seem the friend himself; for almost anything may be more complete and more vivid than our indwelling picture of him.

All this would be different if we visualised perfectly. At the mention of a friend's name

we should see him almost as if he were present
—nay, more—as we have seen him at a hundred significant moments. Not one, but a
thousand sweet shades of himself hover past,
each greeting us as our friend; and at will, as
mood inspires, we fix upon this or that as his
best and faithfullest lieutenant in our affection.
Should we still care for the mere reproduction
of his likeness? Granting that the reproduction, as such, were perfect, it would be one, and
only one, moment in the flux of his life. Any
other instant would represent him perhaps
equally well. But does the single moment
represent him at all? Even the single images
we have of him each take colour and warmth
from the others. The mere reproduction of
our friend would hardly please us, because it
could convey one only of his manifold aspects,
an aspect which, even then, would be inferior
to any one single image of him in our own
minds. The pleasure in mere likeness is, in
fact, the outcome of a feeble power of visualising, and but for this might never have been
known.

Now conceive of an art that could have had

no purpose in helping out our actual visualising, each one of our images being perfect. What could such an art have done to please us through the channel of our eyes? It still would have had two broad domains, one of which we shall call Illustration, and the other Decoration. Both terms need explanation, if not apology. By Decoration I mean all those elements in a work of art which appeal directly to the senses, such as Colour and Tone; or directly stimulate ideated sensations, such as, for instance, Form and Movement. The word has never deliberately been used in quite so wide a sense; indeed, it is one of the vaguest and least hedged-in terms of our language; but as the tendency for some time past has been to make it designate all in a work of art that is not merely expressive, or academic, or dexterous, we shall not be imposing upon it too hard a burden if we make it convey the full meaning I have given it.

A definition of Illustration now follows as a matter of course: it is all that which, in a work of art, is not Decorative. But this definition is too negative, too verbal, to satisfy. We must make it more concrete.   The current use of the word is at once too comprehensive, and, as I shall try to show, too narrow,   Raphael's illustrations to the Bible in the *loggia* of the Vatican cannot be illustrations in the same sense as are the photographic views which commonly embellish magazine articles on travel.   We all feel the difference ; but in what does it really consist ?   The answer will appear if we stop to consider what each does for us.   The view being a mere reproduction, we regard it as a fact, and not as art at all.   It may give pleasure, but only to such as crave either for knowledge, or for greater precision of visual imagery. Raphael's frescoes reproduce nothing which was ever seen in that precise form in the world about us, either by himself or by anyone else.   They convey no information.   But do they also do nothing for our visualising ?   On the contrary, they stock our minds with images.   Images of what—of scenes that never took place ?   Just so.   But surely these are not the visual images we spoke of a little while ago, which we agreed were but shadows in the mind of things actually seen ?   What then are they ?

ILLUSTRATION 7

Ultimately they also are shadows of things actually seen, but combined, blended, and composed in the artist's mind under the spell of the Bible narrative. The process which went on in Raphael's brain takes place in all of us who visualise with any ease. Every word tends to evoke an image, and as we read we are accompanied by an ever unfolding scroll of vague and evanescent shapes—blendings and fusings of the shadows dwelling within—which correspond to the sense of the phrases. Even if this panorama in our own minds lacked nothing in distinctness, we still should get a certain pleasure from the images conjured up by the same words in another mind ; not, as in the case of very poor visualisers, because we longed for greater precision of imagery, but simply for the reason that the imaginary picture can never be quite the same in any two minds. And what if another mind is stocked with shadows of shapes in themselves superior to those of our individual world ; what if that mind also possesses a more effective power of fusing and blending these images, already more attractive than ours? Let that person read the Old Testament, or contemplate anything that can possibly have its graphic counterpart, and pictures will troop past his mental vision which, could we but see them, would reveal higher conceptions and deeper meanings than we ourselves had found, would thrill us with the contagious presence of an imagination—here and at the moment, at least—richer, warmer, and completer than our own.

But how does a mental picture like this become a work of art? The answer would seem simple enough : before the mental image becomes a work of art it must be copied exactly in marble or on canvas. But *is* that really all? Most people would unhesitatingly say yes. They would define art as the faithful reproduction of things in themselves beautiful, or of the fused and blended images of such things. The old talk of the ideal, the new talk of the temperament, Aristotle and Zola, nestle comfortably in this basket. And the common difficulty, the difference between a photograph and such a work of art as, for example, a portrait by Watts, most people would explain by saying that the one reproduces a single image of a person, the

ILLUSTRATION 9

other reproduces a composite formed by a mind
of exceptional power. And thus great art
would be defined not as the blind imitation of
nature, but as the reproduction of the visual
images haunting great minds.

There are some people, however, who would
not rest happy in this definition. Mere reproduction, they would say, is not art, no matter
how beautiful and exalted the object reproduced. The pleasure this gives, they would
add, is not artistic, but æsthetic in a more general sense, or perhaps only intellectual; and
they would insist on making a difference between a thing in itself beautiful (or a beautiful
mental picture) on the one hand, and a work
of art on the other. They would insist also on
distinguishing between the terms "æsthetic"
and "artistic," allowing the meaning of the first
to include the second, but confining "artistic"
to designate that pleasure only which is derived
from a conscious appreciation of the quality
that makes the difference between objects, or
mental images—in themselves beautiful—and
works of art having the qualities which I have
called Decorative. They would not deny that a

work of art might gain from the character of
the object, or of the mental image reproduced,
but they would uphold that its specific value as
Art was perfectly distinct from, and but slightly
dependent upon, the value of the original.
They would go even farther and say that the
work of art, as such, had comparatively little to
gain from the attractiveness of the object represented, but that the artist could enhance and
glorify almost any object that lent itself to his
treatment. Mere reproductions of things, no
matter how exalted in themselves, no matter
whether of objects in actual existence, or of the
sublimest visions of the sublimest imaginations,
they would speak of as " Literature "—and I,
disagreeing with them only in phrase, as Illustration.

At last we have the definition we have been
seeking. Illustration is everything which in a
work of art appeals to us, not for any intrinsic
quality, as of colour or form or composition,
contained in the work of art itself, but for the
value the thing represented has elsewhere,
whether in the world outside, or in the mind
within. If a work of art have no intrinsic value

ILLUSTRATION 11

whatever, or if we fail to perceive it, for us it is nothing but an Illustration, and it does not matter whether it be drawn, engraved, or coloured on sheets of paper, or painted on a panel or wall. Raphael and Michelangelo, Leonardo and Giorgione, if we perceive in them no qualities except such as, in the realms of actual or ideal things, belong to the images set down in their paintings, are as much mere Illustrators as the hacks who furnish designs for the popular press. In the domain of Illustration, there are, it is true, whole universes of difference between the illustrations of the great men just named and the illustrations of the nameless folk of to-day, but from this point of view they are all mere Illustrators.

"Illustration," as I shall employ the word, is then somewhat narrower, and, at the same time, considerably wider a term than the current use, which confines it to art as subordinated to letterpress. It will exclude mere reproduction of single perceptions of objects, too formless to give pleasure to any but the quite uncultivated, for whom simple recognition is already a delight. It will comprise, on the other hand, the mere reproduction of all those visual images, no matter how elaborate and significant, and no matter in what shapes they are cast, of which the form has no intrinsic merit of its own that we more or less consciously perceive.

II.

Now it is no academic reason which has led me, at the opening of a small book on the Central Italian Painters, to speak of visual images, and to distinguish clearly in the work of art between Decoration and Illustration. It is a steep short-cut—would we had had the leisure to build a broad, gently climbing highway !— which, once bravely over, places us where we shall understand a great deal that otherwise would have for ever puzzled and perplexed us.

What more perplexing, for example, than the veerings of fashion, or even of taste? It makes scornful sceptics of most, and forces upon the few who still believe, the alternative of silence or paradox. *De gustibus non est disputandum* is a maxim no less maintained now than in more barbarous ages. It is true, politeness forbids pushing too far a discussion on matters of taste; but if such questions were of enough consequence to compel attention, and if we could communicate our views without fear of offending, is it so certain that we should arrive at no conclusions? I think not. Fortunately it is not our business here and now to make the perilous attempt. But one thing, at least, must be made clear at once. It is this. The question of preference in art is not at all the same that it is in life. Life makes different demands from generation to generation, from decade to decade, from year to year, nay, from day to day, and hour to hour. Our attention is stretched with the utmost interest toward those things that will help us to satisfy these demands, and with admiration toward those of our fellows who, without crowding or hindering us, have perfectly satisfied them. As the demands, so the objects of our desire and our admiration vary. And as the objects of desire and admiration are altered, so will the subject-matter of the arts change. It cannot be otherwise. But depth of conception and attractiveness of ideal are, as we have seen, all that the greater number of even cultivated

people care for in the arts ; and this being so,
art must either present the current conceptions
and ideals, or fail of a result in which even a
restricted public will take an interest. Now
the fluctuation of the ideal can affect those elements only in the work of art in which the
ideal can be obviously manifest—in the Illustrative part. But this, as we have agreed, is
far from being the whole, or even the more
essential factor in art. There remain all the
Decorative elements which mere change in
ideal can not touch, for the good reason that
the ideal can be adequately presented without them. All, therefore, in the work of art
which distinguishes it from the mere mental
image, all the Decorative elements, the more
essential elements, as I believe, are above the
revolutions of fashion and taste. Ages may
arise which lack even the few who in better
periods have a feeling for Art as distinct from
Illustration or dexterity, and they are ages of
bad taste—not of different taste. Some may
prefer Guido Reni to Botticelli, the Caracci to
Giorgione, and Bouguereau to Puvis de Cha-
vannes, but let them not fancy that their preference rests on artistic grounds. The truth is that

the elements essential to a painting as a work of art are beyond their perception, and that they look in a picture for nothing but a representation of something that would please them in actual life, or perhaps for the exhibition of a kind of skill that they happen to appreciate. (There are a thousand standards whereby one's tastes in matters of actual life may be judged, but as none of them are purely artistic, they are not my concern just here.)

Thus our rough division of the elements that constitute the work of art and divide it into two classes, the one Illustrative and the other Decorative, has already been of service. It has enabled us to distinguish what is subject to change and fashion from what is permanent in the work of art. The Decorative elements, the intrinsic values, are as perdurable as the psychic processes themselves, which, as we have reason to believe, vary only in degree from age to age, but in kind remain the same through all times. But Illustration changes from epoch to epoch with the contents of the mind, the visual part of which it reproduces, and it is as varied as are races and individuals.

· It follows then as a clear conclusion that a

phase of art which contains few if any except
Illustrative elements will tend to pass away
with the ideals it reproduces; also, that if we
do not perceive the Decorative factors in the
work of art (which yet may exist there in spite
of our incapacity) we shall cease caring for it
the moment we are tired of the phase of life
or feeling or thought which it embodies.

III.

And now, for the present at all events, we
can cease from abstractions and definitions,
and turn in earnest to the Central Italian
Painters. They were, as we agreed at the
outset, not always enchanting in colour, and
seldom great in form, yet one or another
branch of their school has ever retained the
attention, I will not say of the most artistic,
but certainly of the most cultivated public.
We shall now understand the reason. The
Central Italian Painters were not only among
the profoundest and grandest, but among the
most pleasing and winning Illustrators that we
Europeans ever have had. They saw and reproduced visions which have embodied the

aspirations, the ideals, of two distinct epochs. Of these epochs, the first, the Middle Age, is so far behind us that to most of us its desires and ideals are no longer comprehensible, and the art which embodies them, losing for all but a few whatever glamour and spell it once had as Illustration, has faded into the dulness of documents recording dead things. But in the other epoch we are living still, and the forms which first expressed its cravings and aspirations answer as well to-day as when they were conceived in the mind of Raphael, four hundred years ago.

We shall begin with that school of Central Italian painting which illustrates the Middle Ages. The practice in Italy of the graphic arts had probably never been interrupted since the early days of their origin, and it would be a tedious task to pursue their course through-out its whole length, now stagnating, then dwindling, and finally almost disappearing, until they gushed forth again, fed by vigorous unsearched springs. Was it Etrurian genius reviving? Was it wafted over seas from By-zantium, or did it come from over the mountains, from the smiling fields of France? **Let** historians find answers to these fascinating questions. For our interest lies not in the origin, but in the enjoyment of the work of art, and for enjoyment it is enough to know that painting as an art was flowering toward the end of the thirteenth century within the walls of " soft Siena," then, as always, sorceress and queen among Italian cities.

The first flower of this new growth, the flower from whose seed all Sienese art sprung, was Duccio di Buoninsegna. For this reason, and because he was so typical of his time and school, and anticipated so much that was characteristic of all Central Italian Painters—for all these considerations, we must dwell on him at some length.

All that the Mediæval mind demanded of a painter, Duccio perfectly fulfilled. It was the chief business of the Mediæval artist to re-write the stories of the Saviour, and of His immaculate Mother, in pictographs so elaborate that even the most unlettered could read them. At the same time these pictographs were intended to be offered up as a sacrifice, along with all the rest of the furnishing and actual decoration of God's holy house, and for this they were to be as resplendent as gold and skill could make them. In the hands of a man of genius the pictograph could transform itself into great Illustration, and the sacrifice into great Decoration. Did they suffer this change at the hands of Duccio?

Let us look for answer at the paintings on the reredos that once enclosed with splendour the altar of as proud a temple as Christendom could show. Now it moulders away in the museum outside the Cathedral of Siena, without interest for men, and consequently no longer a fit sacrifice to God. Their metallic lustre, the green and gold, give to these panels such an aspect of subdued sumptuousness as we expect not from paintings, but from bronze reliefs—from Ghiberti's " Gates of Paradise." For the person who approaches them with all his theories safely put to sleep, and his mind on the alert for the distinguishing notes in what he is about to perceive, there is a glamour compounded of sensuous appeal and spiritual association in the first flash of this

mysterious work. It is like the binding of
some priceless illuminated manuscript, inlaid
with ivory, adorned with gold, and set with
precious stones. As you look closer, it is as
if you had turned the covers of a book wherein
you behold a series of splendid Illustrations.
The long-familiar stories are here retold with
a simplicity, a clearness, and a completeness
that, alongside of the blurred images these
tales usually evoked, must have seemed to
most of Duccio's contemporaries like the buoyant sparkle of the morning after groping dark.
And not this alone : Duccio did not merely
furnish the best attainable pictographs. He
gave the stories he told all the value that he,
as a man of genius, felt in them ; he lifted his
spectators to his own level of perception.

Let us glance at a few of these scenes. In
a palace at the end of two rows of pondering,
thought-vexed greybeards, sits a majestic boy.
On the left a woman and an old man entering
lift up their hands in amazement and reproach.
Never has the story of " Christ among the
Doctors " found a fitter illustration. Not a figure too much ; nothing trivial, yet not a touch

to lift it beyond human sympathy. Attitude, gesture, and expression can do no more for the theme.

Another scene : Christ addresses His disciples before He bends to wash their feet. He sits facing them, hieratic, majestic, and they look as if, though they have known Him long, for the first time He is now revealed to them. Fervour of ecstatic credence, the pathetic yearning to lift one's self up, to comprehend, to make one's own the good manifested for too brief a moment, have perhaps never again been so convincingly rendered. Expression—and be it noted, individual expression, for here are different ages and different temperaments—has never been a more obedient handmaid of the gift for sublime interpretation.

In the next panel we see the disciples looking on while Christ washes Peter's feet. Consternation, almost horror, is on their faces, and incredulity withal, as if they can not believe the evidence of their eyes. Christ is all pity and humility. Peter holds his hand to his head as if to make sure of his own identity.

It would be easy to fill the rest of this little

book with descriptions of the scarcely surpassable triumphs of interpretation and expression
to be met with in this one reredos of Duccio's.
But one or two instances more must suffice.
We see Christ resplendent now in robes all gold,
leaping through the gates of hell to deliver from
limbo the patriarchs and prophets.   They troop
up to the mouth of the black cavern, majestic
greybeards, with the yearning expectancy of
thousands of years lingering on their faces.
Then, on earth, it is Easter Day, and as the
light is breaking over the jagged rocks, the three
Marys approach the tomb, and start back as
they behold its lid swung open and upon it a
white-stoled angel, radiant and glorious.   I
know no more impressive rendering of this most
marvellous of all subjects.   To the drama of
expression and gesture, Duccio adds the drama
of light, with all its transfiguring magic.   A
bronzed purple glow flashes through the thin
air, and we feel the vivifying cool of the day-
spring.

Expression, then, and interpretation, grand-
eur of conception, and depth of feeling—the
qualities most essential to great Illustration—

Duccio possessed to the utmost, and this implies that he had sufficient control also of form and movement to render his effects. There remain two other requisites without which the art of Illustration limps rather than leaps. These are Grouping and Arrangement. That Duccio possessed both these in addition to his other gifts we shall be persuaded if we look at several more panels of the Sienese reredos.

Let us turn first to a subject which demands dramatic action and many actors—the " Betrayal of Judas." Motionless, in the middle of the foreground, we see the figure of Christ. The slim and supple Judas entwines Him in an embrace, while the lightly clad soldiers lay hands on Him, the guards crowd round Him, and the Pharisee elders at the sight of His face, which betrays no feeling but pity, start back in horrified consternation. Meanwhile, on the left, hot-tempered Peter rushes at a soldier with his knife, and, on the right, the disciples in a crowded flock scurry away, only the most courageous venturing to look back. We have here two masses of men, and in each the action and expression are kept so clear that to mistake them would imply sheer want of wits. In another panel, representing the "Incredulity of Thomas," Christ, with right arm uplifted, appears baring the wound in His side to the impudent touch of His doubting disciple. These two figures stand out by themselves, and to right and left, more crowded on one side, more scattered on the other, stand the remaining disciples, so arranged that we get the expression on each face.

That Duccio could make us realise space, depth, and distance we must have noticed already while looking at such scenes as the "Marys at the Tomb" or the "Betrayal," but it will not be out of place to add to these a couple of signal instances. First we turn to a bit of *genre* which Duccio has introduced into the midst of all this hieratic solemnity. We see a group of men in the open air huddling about a fire, and bending over with hands outstretched to catch its glow. Peter in the midst is denying Christ, as the serving-maid passes by. While the perspective is far from perfect, we cannot ask for clearer localisation than is here given ; the inner court and chambers, the staircase running up

the side of the house, the space where the men
are sitting,—all are perfectly detached from
one another, and each has ample depth.

Yet another panel, in some ways Duccio's
masterpiece—the " Entry into Jerusalem." We
are in a garden, and as we look over the low
wall to the highroad, we behold Christ followed
by His disciples mounting the paved way. Little boys bearing palm branches and sprigs of
olive march ahead, roguishly looking back, and
meet the crowd streaming through the grand
city gate. On the other side of the highroad
we see an orchard with people clambering up
its high walls and climbing its trees. Beyond
are the Temple and the towers of Jerusalem.
Not only are we made to realise the space in
which all this takes place, but—and this is extraordinary—we are compelled to take a fixed
position as spectators of the scene, and thus are
not only brought in intimate relation to it, but
are obliged to become aware of, to attend to,
the space as space.

It is clear then that Duccio could turn the
pictographs, which for centuries pious souls had
gone on deciphering, into Illustrations that

extracted and presented all the significance sacred story owned, at least in the Mediæval
mind. But was he equally successful in giving
his visual conceptions an intrinsic value beyond
their merit as Illustrations? Are, in Duccio's
work, the Decorative elements, all that they
must be in order that the skilfully transcribed
visual image may be lifted into the realm of
real art? This is the enquiry we must now
pursue.

On first looking at his reredos, we were struck
by the glamour of its subdued refulgence.
Touching us as the gold of old mosaics touches
us, to which time has added a tinge of bronze,
Duccio's panels attune our mood for the enjoyment of whatsoever they may present. This is
doubtless direct and intrinsic, and yet it has
small value from an artistic standpoint; for the
pleasure thus derived rises but little above that
which the mere material itself would give. You
would get as much and more from old gold-
smith's work, from old stuffs, or from old
embroideries. The sensation is still too undif-
ferentiated to be of moment in those arts which,
like painting, depend but slightly upon materials

in themselves pleasurable.   But, as we looked
closer at Duccio's pictures, we noticed certain
qualities essential to good Illustration, which,
as we shall now see, have great Decorative
value also.   How admirably Duccio makes us
realise space, we have observed but now, and
we can here forego returning to the subject.
That it is a quality, however, too specifically
artistic to be required by mere Illustration,
the work of most illustrators of our century,
whether popular or profound, could prove.

In yet another respect we have already found
Duccio eminent,—in his grouping.   We have
dealt with it hitherto only in so far as it concerned clearness of rendering ; but Duccio went
farther, and so grouped as to produce effects of
mass and line, pleasant to the eye in and by
themselves, and pleasantly distributed within
the space at his command.   In other words, he
composed well.   A few examples will make
my meaning clear.   In one or two panels, we
have already noted the arrangement for its
value as Illustration ; we now shall see that it
has still greater merit.   The "Incredulity of
Thomas," would be brought home to us as a

mere historical episode nearly as well if the masses made by the figures were not so rhythmically divided, if a façade of just the right size and shape did not give the entire group the exact background it needed. The expression of Christ and His attitude would have been no different if He did not stand directly under the peak of a pediment, whose height magnifies His own stature, or were not seen against an arched door, which frames Him in, and separates Him from the bystanders, thus making Him more strikingly the centre of attention. Nor, as the mere telling of a tale, would much have been lost if the composition were comprised in a square, instead of being on a panel, that begins, halfway up its height, to slope inward, thus emphasizing those lines of the sloping roof, which have, in their turn, given distinction to the figure of Christ. Even with all this, the sloping lines of the panel might have been continued until they met high above in a peak. But this would have had many unhappy results, among them one most unhappy. The centre of attention, the point at which all the lines tend to converge, would

no longer have been the head of Christ, but a
spot high above Him in the pediment. There
would have been a conflict between the inclin-
ation of our eyes to rest on the spot marked
out for them by the tendency of the dominant
lines, and the desire of our hearts to dwell in
rapt contemplation upon the point of highest
spiritual interest, the face of Christ. This picture, then, does much besides telling its story:
it is a Composition so subtle in its effects of
mass and line that we shall scarcely find its like,
—at least outside the works of one other artist,
that artist also a Central Italian, and holding
the place among the Renaissance masters of
that region which Duccio held among those of
the Middle Ages—I refer of course to Raphael.

Let it not be believed that I have chosen the
one and only instance in which Duccio is a
great composer. There is scarcely a painting
of his which does not betray a sense no less
delicate, if at all, for mass and line and enclos-
ure. Want of space, and the fear of vexing
the reader with descriptions which, to be exact,
should be couched in the jangling vocabulary
of geometry, restrain me from giving many

further examples. But let me refer to one with
which we already are familiar, the "Betrayal
of Judas." What compactness and dignity are
given to the mass in which we find Christ, by
the two tufted trees that surmount it! Without them, the group would look dwarfed and
heavy. Note that the most important figure
here, that of Christ, stands directly under one
of these trees, which occupies the middle of the
whole composition. See how this tree serves,
not only to converge all the lines upon His
head, but helps, by being in continuous upward
movement with Him, to heighten His figure.
And what a glamour of beauty is lent to the
scene by the lances and torches of the soldiers
—lines that are and are not parallel—an effect
so easily attained, yet counting for so much,
not only here, but in numerous compositions
ranging through art, from the Pompeian " Battle of Alexander " to the "Lancers" of Velasquez!

If Duccio was so sublime in his conceptions,
so deep in feeling, so skilful in transcribing
them in adequate forms; if, in addition to all
these merits as an Illustrator, he can win us

with the material splendour of his surfaces; if
he composes as few but Raphael, and can even
make us realize space, why have we heard of
him so seldom, why is he not as renowned as
Giotto, why is he not ranked with the greatest
painters? Giotto was but little younger, and
there could have been a scarcely perceptible
difference between the public of the one and
the public of the other. Most of Giotto's paintings now existing were, in fact, executed rather
earlier than Duccio's reredos. Is the illustrative part of Giotto's work greater? On the
whole, it certainly is not; at times it is decidedly
inferior, seldom having Duccio's manifold ex-
pressiveness, and delicately shaded feeling. If
Giotto, then, was no greater an Illustrator than
Duccio, and if his illustrations, as illustrations,
correspond no more than Duccio's to topics we
crave nowadays to see interpreted in visual
form, and if, as interpretation, they are equally
remote from our own conception and feeling;
if, in short, one is no more than the other a
writer of pictorial leaders on the entrancing
interests of the hour, why is the one still a living force, while the other has faded to the

shadow of a name?   There must exist surely a *viaticum* which bears its possessor to our own hearts, across the wastes of time—some secret that Giotto possessed, and Duccio had never learned.

What is this mysterious life-conserving virtue,—in what does it consist?   The answer is brief—*in life itself*.   If the artist can cunningly seize upon the spirit of life and emprison it in his paintings, his works, barring material accidents, will live forever.   If he contrives to give range to this spirit, to make it leap out, to mingle with and increase the life in our veins, then for as long as we remain humanised beings, he will hold us in his thrall.

I have attempted elsewhere to explain what is this *viaticum*, this quality so essential to the figure arts that, for want of it, when scarcely born, they dwindle away; and to the few short pages of my *Florentine Painters* wherein the question is discussed, I must refer the reader.   Here I shall limit myself to saying that, by means of their more subtle Decorative elements, the arts must be life-enhancing—not by their material charm alone, still less by their

attractiveness as Illustrations. This particular
life-communicating quality is in the figure arts
to be attained by the rendering of form and
movement. I prefer to the word "form" to
use the expression "tactile values," for form
in the figure arts gives us pleasure because it
has extracted and presented to us the corporeal
and structural significance of objects more
quickly and more completely than we—unless,
indeed, we also be great artists, or see as they
see—could have grasped them by ourselves.
This intimate realisation of an object comes to
us only when we unconsciously translate our
retinal impressions of it into ideated sensations
of touch, pressure, and grasp—hence the phrase
" tactile values." Correct drawing, fine modelling, subtle light and shade are not final goods.
In themselves they have no value whatever,
and it does not in the least explain the excellence of a picture to say it is well modelled,
well lighted, and well drawn. We esteem these
qualities because with them the artist succeeds
in conveying tactile values and movement ; but
to suppose that we love pictures merely because they are well painted, is as if we said that

3

we like a dinner because it is well cooked, whereas, in fact, we like it only because it *tastes* good. To speak of the drawing, the modelling, the chiaroscuro, as to speak of cookery in the instance of a dinner, is the business of the persons who paint and cook; but we whose privilege it is to enjoy what has been cooked or painted for us—we, I say, must either talk of it in terms of enjoyment and the psychology thereof, or—talk nonsense!

Tactile values and movement, then, are the essential qualities in the figure arts, and no figure-painting is real,—has a value of its own apart from the story it has to tell, the ideal it has to present,—unless it conveys ideated sensations of touch and movement. If I may be pardoned a very childish parable, it is like some one who comes to us with a message. He tells us something we are very eager to know. No matter how we have been rejoiced by his news, no matter how attractive he seems, if he is merely a messenger, it is only of his message that we think. But let him be a man of character and a gentleman, let him be sympathetic, and his message will have been but the happy accident that has initiated a life-long friendship. And so with a picture; long after, years after we have exhausted its message, if it have tactile values and movement, we are more in love with it than ever, because these qualities, as the attractions in a friend, have the power of directly enhancing life.

And now to return to Duccio. His paintings do not possess these virtues, and therefore have been nearly forgotten, while Giotto's works contain them to a degree so remarkable that even to-day the real lover of art prefers them to all but a very few masterpieces. For Duccio, the human figure was in the first place important as a person in a drama, then as a member in a composition, and only at the last, if at all, as an object whereby to stimulate our ideated feelings of touch and movement. The result is that we admire him profoundly as a pictorial dramatist, as a Christian Sophocles, somewhat astray in the realm of painting; we enjoy his material splendour and his exquisite composition, but rarely if ever do we find him directly life-communicating.

A few instances will prove my point, and I

choose them among subjects which not only
lend themselves to specifically pictorial treatment, but even seem to suggest such treatment
on Duccio's part.   Let us turn again to the
now familiar " Incredulity of Thomas."   That
it appeals to our hearts and minds we were
more than convinced when we studied it as
Illustration ; that it causes the optic muscles
and the mental activities directly dependent on
them to function delightfully, we found while
admiring it as Composition ; but there we stop.
The figures have not even the effectiveness for
evoking sensations of touch and movement
that things bodily present possess, and yet art
should be *more* evocative than actuality.   Look
at Thomas.   As long as you regard him as a
mere shape in a given attitude and with a given
action, he probably corresponds to reality more
than do your visual images, and you find him
pleasant.   But once look for something within
this shape, and you will be surprised, for you
will find not, it is true, a complete lack of tactile values, but only just enough to make the
figure pass as a familiar shape and no more.
Thomas is draped in the very best way for

enabling one to realise his corporeal and func-
tional significance, but unfortunately—although
he is perhaps the best modelled figure in Duccio's entire works—there is not enough under
his robe even to persuade one of reality, not
to speak of stimulating one's own internal
activities; and as for the action, it is scarcely
indicated at all. He certainly seems to move,
yet the legs have not the slightest existence
under the drapery, admirably arranged as it is
to indicate the action of the limbs it ought to
cover; and the feet, while sufficiently resembling feet, have almost no weight and certainly
do not press down on the ground. As a consequence we get none of those ideated sensations of movement and pressure in our own
legs and feet—sensations which, when we feel
them, not only convince us of the reality of the
object that has stimulated them, but give us
much of the pleasure of activity with none of
its drawbacks and fatigues. If we look at the
Christ in this same composition, we find that
He does not stand at all; and it is almost as
bad with another figure which, for mere shape
and attitude has all the qualities of the "Sopho-

cles " of the Lateran. In the panel which represents the " Denial of Peter," we found the story told with the familiarity of *genre*, and even with a touch of humour; yet here again, except for their heads and hands, the figures seem manufactured of tissue paper. None of the bodies suggest resistance to push, they have no weight, they do not settle or press down as they sit, although the artist reproduces well the mere shapes of people in the attitude of sitting and stretching to warm themselves. In the " Washing of the Feet," we see one of the younger disciples half kneeling, half sitting, with his arms stretched down to take off his sandals. Here again, the shape and attitude are well reproduced, and they happen to be such as a great artist would have chosen for the splendid opportunity they afford to render tactile values and movement. But alas! tissue-paper clothes are all we get. Look at the " Miraculous Draught." Three of the disciples have to perfection the facial expression and the attitudes and gestures of people pulling up a heavy weight, but nothing could be flatter and emptier than the figure of just that disciple

who is making the greatest effort. Even the
net is scarcely given any weight, and the fish
inside neither struggle nor sprawl—are not yet
aware that they are in its meshes.

It is a thankless task demonstrating the failings of a great man, and one instance more shall
suffice. Again it is a subject which affords un-
surpassable opportunities for rendering tactile
values and movement,—the "Deposition from
the Cross." A more pathetic, a more felt, a
more dignified version of this theme does not
exist, and Duccio has arranged it as if to go
even farther. An elderly disciple, with his foot
firmly planted on the ladder, and one arm
hooked over the beam of the cross, supports
with the other arm the body of Jesus as it falls
forward lifeless into His Mother's embrace.
Meanwhile, another disciple, kneeling, draws
out the nails from Christ's feet while still they
are fixed to the cross, and yet another disciple
clasps the body about the waist to prevent its
falling forward too far. As mere shape, Christ's
body is a much finer nude than any Giotto ever
painted; nor could the attitudes and gestures
of limp helplessness be better expressed: yet

nothing really happens, There are no tactile values; nothing has the weight wherewith to fall; the arms and hands do not really support —and all for a very good reason. The reason is that, even if Duccio felt tactile values and movement, here, at least, he was so pre-occupied with the facial expression that he could not attend to them.

A question suggests itself at this point, which requires at least a brief answer. If, as results from all that we have just now been observing, Duccio either had no feeling for tactile values and movement, or was too busy elsewhere to attend to them, why has he chosen attitudes and actions which seem to suggest an absorbing interest in them? Surely, for mere Illustration, for mere Composition, for mere material charm,—the qualities in which we have found him great—other arrangements of the figures would have done as well; and how does it happen that he has preferred precisely the arrangements which an artist would have chosen whose dominant interest lay in the presentation of directly life-communicating elements?

The answer is, I think, simple. Duccio did

not choose them, but found them ready made, probably the entire compositions, certainly the single figures; for it is, to me at least, inconceivable that a painter who had perhaps no feeling for tactile values and movement, and certainly no interest in rendering them, should have invented motives valuable chiefly as opportunities for modelling and action. Duccio, I repeat, must have found these motives ready and used them, not for what their inventors had valued in them, but for the mere shapes and attitudes as dramatic factors in Illustration. * To him,

* I am not writing a history of art, and I need not here enter into the question of Duccio's origin and education as an artist; but I owe a word to the curious reader. Duccio must have got his training from some Byzantine master, perhaps at Constantinople itself. Whoever and wherever this master was, he must have been imbued with the feelings of that extraordinary revival of antique art which began at Byzantium in the ninth, and lasted on into the thirteenth century. Duccio, properly regarded, is the last of the great artists of antiquity, in contrast to Giotto, who was the first of the moderns. Duccio's motives, types, and attitudes are still the old art-alphabet of Hellas, made cursive and somewhat debased. His old men are the last descendants, in unbroken line, of the Alexandrian philosophers : his angels, of Victories and Genii ; his devils, of Silenus. As Giotto compares with Giovanni

then, form and movement—the two most essential elements in the figure arts—had no real
meaning of their own.   He exploited them as a
dilettante, but did not understand their real
purpose; and herein again Duccio, the first of
the great Central Italian Painters, was singularly like the last of them; for Raphael also saw in
tactile values and movement not the principal
pursuit of the artist, but a mere aid to Illustration.

IV.

Such, then, was Duccio.   Had he been less,
it might have been better for the art of Central
Italy; for then either a painter of perchance
more talent would have had room to expand
freely, or else the example of Giotto would
have been more attractive.   Duccio, however,
not only trained his followers to conceptions

Pisano, so does Duccio with Giovanni's father, Niccolo, only
that Duccio was far more subtly antique.

Since writing this I have had great pleasure in finding
similar views regarding Duccio's education expressed by Dr.
J. P. Richter, the only critic of our day who adds to a
profound knowledge of Italian art a thorough acquaintance
with the art of Byzantium.

and methods necessarily his own, but by furnishing to an emotional people such as the Sienese
an art that appealed to the feelings, he compelled the painters who came after him to deal
in that perniciously popular article, expressive
Illustration.

It is quite conceivable that if Simone Martini had had for master a painter less powerful
than Duccio, the example of Giovanni Pisano—
excepting perhaps Donatello, the most de-
termining influence in all Italian art,—the example of Giovanni Pisano, and of Giotto, with
both whose works he certainly was acquainted,
would have roused him to a sense of the real
issues in the creation of a work of art. In him
we might have had another painter with Giotto's
feeling for both tactile values and for the mate-
rially significant, but with different ideals to
reveal and a different message to convey.

But Simone had behind him an art, as Illustration so perfectly satisfying both to himself
and to his townsmen, as Decoration so adequate,
far though it was from perfect, that it would
have taken overwhelming genius—if, even then
the conditions of a mediæval town had permit-

ted it—to transcend them and start afresh. There was no departing from Duccio's moulds, in so far as they existed, and individual temperament could manifest itself only by chiselling on the casts that had come out of them.

That Simone felt hampered by Duccio's precedent we see clearly in such works as show him in close rivalry with his master, and it is therefore not in the more dramatic and passionate Gospel themes—themes in which Duccio excelled—that we shall discover Simone's peculiar greatness. In this field Duccio had carried expression to its utmost limits. To retrench on this domain would have been most unacceptable, and the only alternative for one who would not copy, was to leap over the widest limits of artistic expression into the outer waste of mere Illustration. In his scenes from the Passion, Simone, so much above Duccio even there in tactile values, in movement, in charm, falls far below him in dramatic rendering, sacrificing the restraint and severity needed for conveying the real significance of the world-tragedy to the obvious portrayal of facile emotion.

Even when he is freed from Duccio's example, it is not as an artist with a feeling for the
solemnity of actions which have almost a sacra-
mental import that Simone reveals himself.
The charm, the beauty, even the pride of life
attracted him more. For him also painting
was not in the first place an occasion for presenting tactile values and movement, but
equally little was it an opportunity for communicating his sense of moral and spiritual significance. Simone subordinates everything—
and he was great enough to have much to sub-
ordinate—to his feeling for magnificence,
beauty, and grace.

In the Council Hall of Siena we see him in
all his splendour. On one side, radiant in
beauty, the Queen of Heaven sits in the midst
of the noblest of the Saints, the loveliest of the
Virgins, and the sweetest of the Angels. They
hold a more than regal canopy over her head,
they kneel in worship at her feet, they offer
flowers. It is a vision as gorgeous and as elaborate as the façade of Orvieto Cathedral, but
here all is melted into a glow of feeling for
beauty of feature, charm of pose, and loveliness

of colour.   On the opposite wall you see mediæval pride of life incarnate.   It is Guidoriccio
da Fogliano riding through the land.   Horse
and rider are emblazoned with the proud her-
aldry of a long lineage.   How completely
Guidoriccio possesses his steed, how firmly he
holds his commander's staff, with what a level
look he fronts the world !

Then what extraordinary grace of motion and
beauty of line in Simone's miracles of the
Blessed Agostino Novello !   What charm of
feeling in that exquisite fresco at Assisi wherein
we behold the young St. Martin receiving his
knighthood.   The Emperor girds his sword
about the fair youth, a knight fastens his spurs,
while many gay squires look on and listen to
the twanging and piping of the minstrels.   One
of the squires has a profile of the subtlest
beauty, and profiles such as this—nay, more
subtle and mysterious still—are far from rare
in Simone's paintings.   In this small chapel at
Assisi you see types of beauty so strange, so
penetrating, that, far from suggesting our favourite classic or modern ideals, they waft our
thoughts away to Japanese Geishas and Egyptian Queens.

To convey his feeling for beauty and grace and splendour, Simone possessed means more than sufficient. He was master of colour as few have been before him or after him. He had a feeling for line always remarkable, and once, at least, attaining to a degree of perfection not to be surpassed. He understood decorative effects as a great musician understands his instruments. Where shall we see colour more symphonic than in the single figures among his Assisi frescoes! What has line accomplished that can outvie the miraculous contours of his "Coronation of King Robert"! How subtle the beauty, how dainty the movements, how sweet the olive in the Uffizi "Annunciation"! As you look at the angel's mantle it is as if you were seeing the young sunlight on driven snow. Simone is the most lovable of all the Italian artists before the Renaissance.

V.

The native tendency of Sienese art toward mere Illustration, in Duccio was held in bond by a sense for the significant, and by a feeling for all the subtleties of composition. Simone was held back by his love of beauty and his delight in splendour of colour and flow of line. No such check was operative upon the brothers Lorenzetti. Singularly gifted, they display their gifts but listlessly. Beauty, which they felt with passion; form, which Giovanni Pisano and Giotto had so amply revealed to them, even the sense of human significance with which they were aglow, they sooner or later sacrificed, either to the mere representation of things, or to the vain endeavour to body forth dim, infinite meanings.

What fascination they can give to figures yet possessed of the highest dignity and solemnity, we see in Ambrogio's portable altarpiece at Siena, wherein the Madonna, hieratic, Egyptian, sits enthroned in the midst of Virgins, glowing like flames, and ancient saints yearning toward her. Also in the Siena collection you shall see Ambrogio's " Annunciation," where the Blessed Virgin is warm with welcome and gladness as she leans forward to receive the palm of martyrdom which Gabriel brings her with his message. At Assisi, in a fresco by Pietro, of such relief and such enamel as to seem contrived of ivory and gold rather than painted, the Madonna holds back heart-broken tears as she looks fixedly at her Child, who, Babe though He is, addresses her earnestly ; but she remains unconsoled. Nowhere is beauty more penetrating than in Ambrogio's St. Catherine, or earnestness and intellect more convincing than in his Francis or Bernard. And where is there more magic than in that most precious panel of the Florence Academy, in which Nicholas of Myra, standing by the rock-bound sea, fronts the setting sun !

Such artists Ambrogio and Pietro Lorenzetti could have been always had they not made the great refusal. But Pietro sank to such rubbish as his Passion scenes at Assisi, where he carries Duccio's themes to the utmost pitch of frantic feeling. Form, movement, composition,—even depth and significance,— all have been sacrificed to the expression of the most obvious and easy emotion. Such anarchy has seldom again overtaken an Italian master, even of the Bolognese School. To find its like you must go to Spain and to certain Germans.

4

As for Ambrogio, the more gifted of the brothers, his fall was scarcely less. At his worst he hardly surpasses the elder Breughel. He seems to have itched to reproduce whatsoever he saw. Having to paint frescoes symbolizing Good and Bad Government, he makes no attempt to extract the essence of these conceptions and to clothe them in forms which must needs convey them to us. Giotto, in two or three figures, could make us not only grasp with our minds what good and bad government are, but realise them with our bodies. Ambrogio Lorenzetti could think of nothing but vast panoramas overshadowed by figures powerless to speak for themselves, and obliged to ply us with signs and scrolls. Scores and scores of episodes—some of them charming when taken alone—depict with remorseless detail what happens in town and country when they are well or ill governed. You look at one after another of these episodes, and you get much information about the way of living at Siena in the fourteenth century, and a certain sum of pleasure from the quaintness, and even the skill, with which it has all been done;

but none of that life-enhancement which comes
with the vivid apprehension of thoughts and
feelings vaster and deeper than our own. And
matters are not mended when even vaguer
allegory is attempted. If the frescoes just
described are little more than a painted char-
ade, certain compositions of the Lorenzetti are
no better than a rebus. And with this depart-
ure from artistic intention, there went, as a
matter of course, a decline in artistic value.
First to disappear utterly was composition ;
then the never too strong feeling for tactile
values and movement ; finally, even the sense
of beauty left them in disdain.

But in an age wherein Italy was almost as
troubled and as wistful as Germany two centuries later, the works of the Lorenzetti, with
their turbid outpourings of uncouth yearnings,
had the kindling effect of those fly-leaf engravings that so powerfully stirred the later age—
with which indeed their art had much in common. Finding fit substance, they once or twice
fanned into flame talents actually surpassing
their own.

Such a talent was that of the painter in the

Campo Santo at Pisa, who has left as the great
trace of his activity, the famous "Triumph of
Death," as mere Illustration, by far the greatest
Italian achievement of the Middle Ages.   Endowed with more feeling for the essential problems in painting than the Lorenzetti, he yet
follows them closely in moral and philosophical
purpose.   He has a sense of form, a command
of movement, not common at any time; he
has a plastic fancy, and a power of giving real
feature and life to his dream, rarer still.   His
devils and goblins—herein so different from the
rabble of such representations—are not feebly
and ludicrously quaint, but alive and endowed
with the hard-won beauty of the true grotesque.   His Death would be terrifyingly recognisable even without the bat's wings and the
scythe.

All these talents the unknown painter of
these frescoes sacrificed, as in our day Maupas-
sant, Ibsen, and Tolstoi have done, to the presentation of glaring contrasts for the pure joy
thereof, or to the teaching of maxims absorb-
ingly new yesterday, tediously trite to-morrow.
Aside from its artistic qualities, the "Triumph

of Death " is made up of two contrasts. Under shady trees, in a bower, a gay company of knights and ladies solace their hours with music and love. It would not be difficult to describe this scene in language most modern, but the reader who wishes to preserve its glamour, and who yet must have a text, should read the opening pages of Boccaccio's *Decameron*. Outside, the pest is raging and the crumbling lepers stretch their vain hands towards Death, who, heedless of their lamentation, swoops down upon the merry bower. Here is contrast enough. Surely there is no more in " *La Maison Tellier*." But it did not seem sufficient to the artist, and he repeats the tale in even clearer language. The pride and joy of life, cavaliers and ladies, a cheerful hunting party are breathing the morning air. Suddenly their horses start back, their dogs snarl, their own hands go to their noses. They have come upon rotting carcasses of kings and prelates. This time surely the contrast must be enough. But no! Our painter did not credit us with sufficient intelligence, and an officious hermit presents a text on a scroll. And then we become aware that the fresco is full of texts on scrolls.   What an artist, and what must he have thought of his public!

VI.

With the death of the Lorenzetti, the Sienese school of painting fell into a decline from which it never earnestly rallied.   It had moments of hopefulness and hours of hectic beauty, but never again did it receive that replenishment of force without which art is doomed to dwindle away.   Barna, Bartolo di Fredi, and Taddeo di Bartolo at times catch a glow from the splendour of Simone Martini and the Loren-zetti; and Domenico di Bartolo made an un-couth attempt to breathe new life into the school, to replenish it by introducing the shapes and attitudes which the great Florentines had just saved out of chaos and forever fixed.   But as he felt not at all the real significance of these new forms and new gestures (as serving to render either tactile values or movement), his fellows in craft and town had the taste to prefer, to the mock-heroics of a misunderstood naturalism, the unsubstantial but lovely shapes of their long-hallowed tradition.   The ever

winsome Sano di Pietro lived and painted as if
Florence were not forty but forty millions of
miles away, as if Masaccio and Donatello, Uccello and Castagno had not yet deserted the
limbo of unborn babes. And he has made us
the richer by many works of rich, decorative
beauty, and by that scene of visionary splendour, the Chantilly " Marriage of the Seraphic
St. Francis."

But stealthily and mysteriously the new visual imagery, the new feeling for beauty, found
its way into Siena, though it had to filter
through those frowning walls. And the old
feeling for line, for splendid surface, for effects
rudimentally decorative, mingled with the new
ideals. Painters of this newness were Vecchietta,
Francesco di Giorgio and Benvenuto di Giovanni, and, finer than these, Matteo di Giovanni
and Neroccio di Landi, the two greatest masters of Renaissance Siena. Matteo had a feeling for movement which would have led to
real art if he had had the necessary knowledge of form ; lacking this, he became an inferior Crivelli, giving us effects of firm line cut in
gilt cordovan or in old brass. As for Neroccio

—why, he was Simone come to life again. Simone's singing line, Simone's endlessly refined feeling for beauty, Simone's charm and grace—you lose but little of them in Neroccio's panels, and you get what to most of us counts more, ideals and emotions more akin to our own, with quicker suggestions of freshness and joy.

Then it was already the end of the fifteenth and the beginning of the sixteenth century, and even the Sienese could no longer be satisfied with the few painters who remained in their midst. Masters were summoned from without, Signorelli, Pintoricchio, and Perugino from Umbria, Fra Paolino from Florence, Sodoma from Lombardy; and as there were no forces at home to offer sufficient resistance, there resulted from all these mingled influences a most singular and charming eclecticism—saved from the pretentiousness and folly usually controlling such movements by the sense for grace and beauty even to the last seldom absent from the Sienese.

VII.

The school of Siena fails to rank among the great schools of art because its painters never devoted themselves with the needed zeal to form and movement. They preferred to give body to their dream, to record the visual images teeming in their minds. But little as the specifically artistic elements, those which are neither Illustrative nor rudimentarily Decorative, are prized at any time, the visual images evoked by the faded ideals and vanished longings of a past epoch are wanted still less. The very way of visualising has so changed since the full flood of the Renaissance set in, that to most of us the forms of the fourteenth-century painters are little more than grotesque. We hail in them no goal for our own groping efforts to body forth familiar shapes. They remain, as far as we are concerned, in the realm of curiosity, and never, by such stimulating of more rapid processes of consciousness as Illustration of a nearer epoch gives, do they enhance life. For so deeply inrooted is the gross fallacy that art is the mere reproduction of an actual or ideal reality, that, unless we recognise such a reality in a picture, most of us will look no farther.

This is not the place to discuss in detail the relation of visual images to the objects they reflect—a question, however, which I trust may some day be carefully studied by psychologists. Whatever be their relation in a world where art does not exist, in civilised men this relation is certainly much determined by the works of art surrounding them. For nature is a chaos, indiscriminately clamouring for attention. Even in its least chaotic state it has much more resemblance to a freakish and whirlingly fantastical " Temptation of St. Antony " by Bosch, than to such compositions by Duccio as I have already described, or such others by Raphael as we shall look at later. To save us from the contagious madness of this cosmic tarantella, instinct and intelligence have provided us with stout insensibility and inexorable habits of inattention, thanks to which we stalk through the universe tunnelled in and protected on every hand, bigger than the ants and wiser than the bees. And such superior brute beasts we should be, no more, no less, but for that Garden of Eden which is Art, and Science, its serpent-haunted Tree. For art is a garden cut off from chaos wherein there is provided, not only an accord like that of the beasts between our physical needs and our environment, but a perfect attuning of the universe to our entire state of consciousness. In one point alone is the unknown author of the Book of Genesis in the wrong. Too narrow in his devotion to art, as is the wont of critics, he regarded the Tree of Knowledge as an afterthought, whereas surely knowledge must have existed before there was a Garden ; for the accumulating of facts and the reasoning about them (in no matter how unconscious a form) must precede every endeavour to harmonise them with the needs of the human spirit. Eden is really begotten of the Tree of Knowledge, whereof Art is but the flower. It is the Serpent, misunderstood and maligned by the narrow æstheticism of the writer of Genesis, who nurses the fruit which will, in its turn, produce other trees blossoming into other Edens ; for the Serpent is the symbol of mental energy forever at work.

But to speak plainly—the most difficult thing in the world is to see clearly and with one's own eyes, naïvely. What with the almost numberless shapes assumed by an object, which shapes only we see, but never a form perfectly expressing the object itself ; what with our insensitiveness and inattention, things scarcely would have for us features and outlines so determined and clear that we could recall them at will, but for the stereotyped shapes art has lent them. So invincible a task is the business of learning to see for one's self, that all except the few men of genius—with a gift for seeing— have to be taught how to see. Only when a person is to become an artist is a systematic effort made to teach him. But note how it is done—or at least how, until the other day, it used to be done. He was set to copy simple drawings of his own master, or of other artists. Then the antique was put before him, and he had to copy that. By this time his habits of vision were well on the way to becoming fixed, and, unless he were endowed with unusual powers of reacting against teaching, he passed the rest of his life seeing in objects only those shapes and forms that the drawings and antiques put before him had pointed out to him. How difficult, in the result, it still is to see may be gathered from the extensive use of the photographic camera among painters, even when copying the works of others!

As for the rest of us, who are not artists by profession, we get no systematic training at all in seeing forms, though we may be well able, owing to natural talent or education in science, to observe detail. The little we learn we pick up from illustrated periodicals and books, from statues, from pictures. And unless years devoted to the study of all schools of art have taught us also to see with our own eyes, we soon fall into the habit of moulding whatever we look at into the forms borrowed from the one art with which we are acquainted. There is our standard of artistic reality. Let anyone give us shapes and colours which we cannot instantly match in our paltry stock of hackneyed forms and tints, and we shake our heads at his failure to reproduce things as we know they certainly are, or we accuse him of insincerity. When, a few years ago, the impressionist *plein-air* painting arose, how still and small were the voices asking whether it was beautiful, how loud and indignant those which denied its truth!

This brings me back to my theme. If we are sufficiently displeased when the painter of to-day does not visualise objects exactly as we do, how remote must we find the art of people who visualised in a way perfectly distinct from our own! To how many of us, for this very reason, are Chinese and Japanese art not art at all. But no less remote to those who have not been trained to appreciate it is the art, or, to be more exact, that part of art which is all most people care for, the Illustration of the Middle Ages. For since then, our manner of visualising forms has changed in a thousand ways.

What brought about this change? In the first place, the Serpent, that restless energy which never allows man to abide long in any Eden, the awakening of the scientific spirit. Then the fact that, by a blessed accident, much, if not most, of this awakened energy was at first turned not to science but to art. The result thereof was Naturalism, which I have defined elsewhere as science using art as the object of its studies and as its vehicle of expression. Now science, devoting itself, as it earnestly did at the beginning of the fifteenth century, to the study of the shapes of things, did not take long to discover that objective reality was not on the side of the art then practised. And, thanks to the existence at that moment of a man not less endowed with force to react against tradition, than with power to see —a power, I believe, unparalleled before or since —thanks to this one man, Donatello, art in an instant wrenched itself free from its immediate past, threw to the winds its whole mediæval stock of images, and turned with ardour and zeal to the reproduction of things as research was discovering them to be. There was scarcely a trace of an ideal remaining. Every man had a shape of his own ; any man therefore was as good for reproducing as another. Why not ? This chaos, or at best the Walt-Whitmanism, to which in the plastic arts mere Naturalism would have led, was prevented, and its force conducted into nourishing channels, by certain other tendencies and impulses then happily prevalent.

Donatello himself was much more than a Naturalist; he was eager with a desire to communicate movement, to express action. He tended therefore, out of the countless shapes which presented themselves, to choose such as would best manifest the play of alert and agile forces. Carried to an extreme, this tendency would have ended in an art more like that of Japan than of modern Europe. That we were not brought to this point is due chiefly to Masaccio, whose controlling instinct was for tactile values. His choice among shapes was of such only as could most readily be made to stimulate ideated sensations of touch—of figures, therefore, tall, broad-shouldered, reservoirs of force and resistance. Whatever danger there was in this of an art too monumental, was, in its turn, counteracted by Donatello's feeling for movement. The resulting canon of the human figure would have been no nearer to the Mediæval, not much farther away from our own, than it now is, if it had remained the mere composite of Donatello and Masaccio. But at the last moment two other influences entered in to fix the canon and make it permanent even to our own day. Antiquity, the dream, the hope, the glamour of the cultivated classes in the fifteenth century, had left behind it a few scattered fragments of its own art. Crude copies though these were, many removes away from their originals, yet—being in the last resort creations of men with almost unrivalled feeling for tactile values, movement, and the relation of the two —they bore a conspicuous resemblance to the new art. And this likeness to antiquity, resulting, not from the imitation of the one by the other, but from kinship of purpose and similarity of material, won over the Humanists —the men of letters and all-powerful journalists of that time—to the art of their contemporaries. Not that they understood the real meaning of the new movement—how could people without a vast experience in the enjoyment of all schools of art do that? Imitation of antiquity was their only thought; they seemed to recognise such an imitation in the new art, and thereupon it received their full sanction. But this was not without evil con-

5

sequences, for, later, as I hope to show elsewhere, the Humanists ended by forcing weaker
spirits to some slight aping of Antiquity.
Great has been their success in spreading the
belief that Renaissance art throughout (not, as
was the case, architecture alone, the other arts
only here and there) was the product of Antiquity imitated.

Created by Donatello and Masaccio, and sanc-
tioned by the Humanists, the new canon of the
human figure, the new cast of features, expressing, because the figure arts, properly used, could
not express anything else, power, manliness,
and stateliness, presented to the ruling classes
of that time the type of human being most
likely to win the day in the combat of human
forces.   It needed no more than this to assure
the triumph of the new over the old way of
seeing and depicting.   And as the ideals of
effectiveness have not changed since the fifteenth century, the types presented by Renaissance art, despite the ephemeral veerings of
mere fashion and sentiment, still embody our
choice, and will continue to do so, at least as
long as European civilisation keeps the essenti-

ally Hellenic character it has had ever since the Renaissance.

The way of visualising affected by the artists, the Humanists, and the ruling classes could not help becoming universal. Who had the power to break through this new standard of vision and, out of the chaos of things, to select shapes more definitely expressive of reality than those fixed by men of genius? No one had such power. People had perforce to see things in that way and in no other, to see only the shapes depicted, to love only the ideals presented. Nor was this all. Owing to those subtle and most irresistible of all forces, the unconscious habits of imitation, people soon ended either by actually resembling the new ideals, or at all events, earnestly endeavouring to be like them. The result has been that, after five centuries of constant imitation of a type first presented by Donatello and Masaccio, we have, as a race, come to be more like that type than we ever were before. For there is no more curious truth than the trite statement that nature imitates art. Art teaches us not only what to see but what to be.

VIII.

The art of Siena exhausted itself in presenting the ideals and feelings of the Middle Ages
with an intensity and a beauty not surpassed
even by their spiritual kindred, those sculptors
of Northern France who, in our weaker moments,
almost win us away from Greece.   It remained
for another school of Central Italy, the Umbrian,
to carry on through the Renaissance, purposes
and aims nowise different in their essence from
those of Siena, different as they may seem in
actual result.   For Umbrian art, as we shall see,
is, as a whole, no more in earnest over tactile
values and movement than Sienese art had
been, and no less devoted to the task of illus-
trating the ideals and expressing the wistful
desires of the time.

But before we turn to the Umbrians, our attention must first be given to a master and his
two pupils, neither Sienese nor Umbrian, dwell-
ers in Southern Tuscany and the Romagna, who
as men of genius were all greater than any of
the Umbrians, as artists freer and more powerful, if not always so delightful—I mean Piero

dei Franceschi, Luca Signorelli, and Melozzo da Forlì.

And first to Piero. The pupil of Domenico Veneziano in characterisation, of Paolo Uccello in perspective, himself an eager student of this science, as an artist he was more gifted than either of his teachers. He is hardly inferior to Giotto and Masaccio in feeling for tactile values ; in communicating values of force, he is the rival of Donatello; he was perhaps the first to use effects of light for their direct tonic or subduing and soothing qualities ; and, finally, judged as an Illustrator, it may be questioned whether another painter has ever presented a world more complete and convincing, has ever had an ideal more majestic, or ever endowed things with more heroic significance.

Unfortunately he did not always avail himself of his highest gifts. At times you feel him to be clogged by his science, although never, like Uccello, does he suggest the surveyor and topographer rather than the painter. Now and again such as are always on the outlook for their favourite type of beauty, will receive shocks from certain of Piero's men and women.

Others still may find him too impersonal, too impassive.

Impersonality—that is the quality whereby he holds us spell-bound, that is his most distinguishing virtue,—one which he shares with only two other artists: the one nameless, who carved the pediments of the Parthenon, and the other Velasquez, who painted without ever betraying an emotion.

"The impersonality of art"—a phrase not familiar enough to pass without comment. I mean two different things, one a method, the other a quality. As a method, impersonality has been understood by all the great artists and the few competent critics who have ever existed. They have appreciated the fact that in art, as in life, those few among us who have not reduced the whole of the phenomenal universe (or at least all of it that ever concerns us) to a series of mere symbols, those of us whom physical and mental habits have not so crushingly enslaved but that we retain some freedom of perception —they have understood that such people will react to every different object in a different way, no matter how slight the difference. If a given situation in life, a certain aspect of landscape, produces an impression upon the artist, what must he do to make us feel it as he felt it? There is one thing he must not do, and that is to reproduce his own feeling about it. That may or may not be interesting, may or may not be artistic : but one thing it certainly cannot do— it cannot produce upon us the effect of the original situation in life or the original aspect of the landscape ; for the feeling is not the original phenomenon itself, but the phenomenon, to say the least, as refracted by the personality of the artist. And this personal feeling being another thing, must needs produce another effect. The artist will therefore carefully avoid reproducing his own feeling, He will leave himself out of count, and, reducing the original phenomenon to its essential significant facts and forces, will reproduce these, and thus really make us, in our turn, react to them as he has reacted, and feel as he has felt.

That Piero dei Franceschi was impersonal in this sense will be readily granted ; for was he not a great artist? He was, however, impersonal not in his method only, as all great artists are, but he was what would be commonly called impassive, that is to say unemotional, in his conceptions as well. He loved impersonality, the absence of expressed emotion, as a quality in things. Having, for artistic reasons, chosen types the most manly, and, for perhaps similar reasons, a landscape which happens to be of the greatest severity and dignity, he combined and recombined them as each subject required, allowing the grand figures, the grand action, and the severe landscape, these, and these alone, to exercise upon us, as they must when all special emotion is disregarded, their utmost power. He never asks what his actors feel. Their emotions are no concern of his. Yet no " Flagellation " is more impressive than one of his, although you will not find on the face of any of the *dramatis personæ* an expression responsive to the situation ; and, as if to make the scene all the more severely impersonal, Piero has introduced into this marvellous picture three majestic forms who stand in the very foreground as unconcerned as the everlasting rocks. And so, in his fresco of the " Resurrection," Piero has not even thought of asking himself what type of person Christ was. He chose one of the manliest and most robust, and in the grey watered light of the morning, by the spreading cypresses and plane trees, you see this figure rising out of the tomb. You feel the solemnity, the importance of the moment, as in perhaps no other version of this subject; and, if you are a person sensitive to art, you will have felt all this before you have thought of asking whether Christ looks appropriately Christ-like, or whether there is a fit expression on His face.

The spell of an art as impersonal, as un-emotional as Piero's (or that of Velasquez) is undeniably great, but why is it—in what does its charm, its potent attractiveness consist? It is, I think, a compound of many things. In the first place, where there is no specialised expression of feeling—so attractive to our weak flesh —we are left the more open to receive the purely artistic impressions of tactile values, movement, and chiaroscuro. So unnecessary do I find facial expression, and indeed, at times so disturbing, that, if a great statue happens to be without a head, I seldom miss it; for the forms and the action, if both be adequate, are expressive enough to enable me to complete the figure in the sense that they indicate; while there is always a chance that the head, in works of even the best masters, will be over-expressive —in a direction either not necessitated by the forms and action, or in flat contradiction to them.

But there is another reason, less artistic and more general, to account for the effect of impassiveness in art.   As ardently as we love those beings who react to things by the measure and in the quality that we ourselves react to them, so, in other moods, in moments of spent sensibility, we no less eagerly love those other beings or objects which, though we endow them with a splendid and kindred personality, yet do not react at all to things that almost overpower us. Taking it for granted that they are no less sensitive than we are, and seeing that they are not moved at all where perhaps we should be overwhelmed, we ascribe to them the calm and majesty of heroes; and as we more than half become the things we admire, we also, for a moment too brief, are heroes.   This sentiment, when exaggeration does not make it Byronic, becomes such an attitude toward landscape as

Wordsworth's, such an attitude toward man as Piero dei Franceschi's. The artist, depicting man disdainful of the storm and stress of life, is no less reconciling and healing than the poet who, while endowing Nature with Humanity, rejoices in its measureless superiority to human passions and human sorrows.

IX.

Piero was followed by two pupils, Melozzo, and Signorelli, each of whom, starting with the heritage Piero left them, and following the promptings of his own temperament, and the guidance of his own genius, touched excellence in his own splendid way. Melozzo was the grander temperament, Signorelli the subtler and deeper mind.

Melozzo took the heroic creations of his master—hearts which an emotion had never visited. He assimilated as much as he thought necessary of Piero's science, the science for which Piero had fought so hard that his paintings too often retain more trace of the battle-ground than are pleasant. These majestic types, and the wonderful knowledge of movement needed to articulate them, Melozzo expended upon a purpose at the farthest remove from Piero's. For Melozzo, the figure was never impassive, never an end in itself, but always a means for embodying emotions. And these emotions are so overpowering, his grandly robust forms are so possessed by them, that personality and even mere awareness are swept clean away, the figures becoming pure incarnations of the one great feeling by which they are animated. Of these feelings his figures would be the concrete symbols, could we ourselves but stand off and regard them at the distance of the intellect. But they carry us away and we also become possessed. You might as well remain indifferent to Calvé where in *Carmen* she is most the sorceress. As abandoned to the one feeling, as unconscious of others, or even of self, as impersonal, are the music-making angels in Melozzo's sacred fragments at St. Peter's. Nor is it Dionysiac rapture only that the master could portray. Nowhere perhaps as in his renowned "Apothecary's Apprentice Pounding Herbs" does painting show such embodiment of the joy in mere living, the play of muscles, and the use of limbs ; and his Prophets (in a sacristy of the

Holy House at Loreto) have a solemnity and magical aloofness such as can be found only in Æschylus and Keats when they speak of fallen dynasties of gods.

Luca Signorelli does not glow with Melozzo's consuming fire; and yet he takes his rank beyond. His was the finer and deeper mind, his genius fetched the larger compass, his perception of value, both in life and in art, was subtler and more just. Even in feeling for the poetry in things, Luca was inferior to no man. Then —to be more specific—to a sense for tactile values scarcely less than Giotto's, Luca added, Masaccio's or Piero dei Franceschi's command over action. In this, indeed, he almost rivalled his own teacher in that art and its unparalleled master, Antonio Pollaiuolo. Great artist he would have been with these qualities alone, but for him they were means to an end, and that end, different from Melozzo's, was his joy in the Nude.

What the Nude is and whence its supereminence in the figure arts, I have discussed elsewhere.* I must limit myself here to the statement that the nude human figure is the

* *The Florentine Painters of the Renaissance.*

only object which in perfection conveys to us values of touch and particularly of movement. Hence the painting of the Nude is the supreme endeavour of the very greatest artists; and, when successfully treated, the most life-communicating and life-enhancing theme in existence. The first modern master to appreciate this truth in its utmost range, and to act upon it, was Michelangelo, but in Signorelli he had not only a precursor but almost a rival. Luca, indeed, falls behind only in his dimmer perception of the import of the Nude and in his mastery over it. For his entire treatment is drier, his feeling for texture and tissue of surface much weaker, and the female form revealed itself to him but reluctantly. Signorelli's Nude, therefore, does not attain to the soaring beauty of Michelangelo's; but it has virtues of its own—a certain gigantic robustness and suggestions of primeval energy.

The reason why, perhaps, he failed somewhat in his appreciation of the Nude may be, not that "the time was not ripe for him," as is often said, but rather that he was a Central Italian—which is almost as much as to say an

Illustrator. Preoccupied with the purpose of conveying ideas and feelings by means of his own visual images, he could not devote his complete genius to the more essential problems of art. Michelangelo also was an Illustrator—alas!—but he, at least, where he could not perfectly weld Art and Illustration, sacrificed Illustration to Art.

But a truce to his faults! What though his nudes are not perfect; what though—as in candour must be said—his colour is not always as it should be, a glamour upon things, and his composition is at times crowded and confused? Luca Signorelli none the less remains one of the grandest—mark you, I do not say pleasantest—Illustrators of modern times. His vision of the world may seem austere, but it already is ours. His sense of form is our sense of form; his images are our images. Hence he was the first to illustrate our own house of life. Compare his designs for Dante (frescoed under his Heaven and Hell at Orvieto) with even Botticelli's, and you will see to what an extent the great Florentine artist still visualises as an alien from out of the Middle Ages, while Signorelli

estranges us, if indeed at all, not by his quaintness but by his grand austerity.

It is as a great Illustrator first, and then as a
great artist that we must appreciate Signorelli.
And now let us look at a few of his works
—works which reveal his mastery over the
nude and action, his depth and refinement of
emotion, the splendour of his conceptions.
How we are made to feel the murky bewil-
derment of the risen dead, the glad, sweet
joy of the blessed, the forces overwhelming the
damned! It would not have been possible to
communicate such feelings but for the Nude,
which possesses to the highest degree the power
to make us feel, all over our own bodies, its own
state. In these frescoes at Orvieto how complete a match for the " Dies Irae " are the skies
with their overshadowing trains of horror, and
the trumpet blasts of the angels! What high
solemnity in his Volterra " Annunciation "—
the flaming sunset sky, the sacred shyness of
the Virgin, the awful look of Gabriel! At Cortona, in an " Entombment," you see Christ up-
held by a great angel who has just alighted from
a blessed sphere, its majesty still on his face,

its dew on his wings. Look at Signorelli's music-making angels in a cupola at Loreto. Almost they are French Gothic in their witchery, and they listen to their own playing as if to charm out the most secret spirit of their instruments. And you can see what a sense Signorelli had for refined beauty, if, when sated with Guido's " Aurora," you will rest your eyes on a Madonna by him in the same pavilion of the Rospigliosi Palace.

The Nude for its own sake, for its distinctly tonic value, was used by Signorelli in one of the few most fascinating works of art in our heritage—I mean his " Pan " at Berlin. The goat-footed Pan, with the majestic pathos of nature in his aspect, sits in the hushed solemnity of the sunset, the tender crescent moon crowning his locks. Primevally grand nude figures stand about him, while young Olympos is piping, and another youth lies at his feet playing on a reed. They are holding solemn discourse, and their theme is " The Poetry of Earth is never Dead." The sunset has begotten them upon the dew of the earth, and they are whispering the secrets of the Great Mother.

6

And now, just a glance at one or two of Luca's triumphs in movement. They are to be found chiefly in his *predelle*, executed in his hoary old age, where, with a freedom of touch at times suggesting Daumier, he gives masses in movement, conjoined, and rippling like chain mail. Perhaps the very best are certain bronzed *predelle* at Umbertide, a village situate upon the Tiber's bank; but more at hand is one in the Uffizi, painted in earlier years, an " Annunciation," wherein the Angel runs so swiftly that he drinks the air before him.

X.

Among the other Central Italians Piero dei Franceschi, Melozzo and Signorelli stand out as conspicuous exceptions, being artists unusually endowed with a feeling for tactile values and movement, and all that by these means may accrue as advantage to art. We shall find no such men among the masters of the third school of Central Italian painting— the Umbrian.

Umbrian painting, when first we meet it, is but a provincial offshoot of Sienese art, the strides of which it followed with timid short steps. Left to itself, it produced such a marsh growth as Ottaviano Nelli's frescoes at Foligno, works of such senile imbecility that Siena, in her most palsied moments, cannot show their equal. Yet Umbria, although succeeding to the aspirations, ideals, and methods of Siena, was not, like that proud city, closed to foreign influences ; and contact, direct or indirect, with Florence gave the Umbrian school not only the wherewithal to pursue its career to a glorious climax, but to do for the Renaissance and subsequent times what Siena had done for the Middle Ages, though it was too feeble and too ignorant to do it again—to pick out from the chaos of things and to fix those images and visions which in actual life would bring gladness and peace, to charge with fresh meanings great themes grown too familiar, to set fresh goals for tireless aspirations, to enshrine in new-made forms a new-felt loveliness.

And to this task, perhaps more priest-like than pictorial, the school of Umbria remained severely faithful. Never once was it won over to art for art's own sake. It remained *dilet-*

tante, with no feeling for form, caring little for movement, using them ready-made, not for their own tonic virtues, but as means to the Illustrator's end.

Umbrian art reveals itself clearly, if not completely, in its first great master, Gentile da Fabriano. To a feeling for beauty, and a sense for colour nurtured on Sienese models, to a power of construction fostered by contact with Florentine art, Gentile added a glowing vivacity of fancy, and, thus prepared, he devoted his life to recording the Mediæval ideal of terrestrial happiness, clear, complete at last (as is the wont of ideals) when the actuality, of which it was the enchanting refraction, was just about to fade into the past. Fair knights and lovely ladies, spurs of gold, jewelled brocade, crimson damasks, gorgeous trains on regal steeds ride under golden skies wherein bright suns flatter charmed mountain tops. All the faces are aglow with blitheness. Why are they so happy? Have they waked from nightmare hauntings of Purgatory and Hell? So it would seem, and they rejoice in the blood tickling their veins, in the cool breezes, in the smell of flowers. And what a love of flowers! Gentile fills with them even the nooks and crannies of the woodwork enframing his gorgeous "Epiphany."

But in Umbria such was the dearth of talent that among his countrymen Gentile found no one to succeed him. (What rich fabrics could be constructed with his ore we may behold in the fascinating achievements of his North Italian pupils, Vittore Pisano and Jacopo Bellini.) The child's prattle of Boccatis, winning at times, but ever crude, is all that languishing Umbrian art can show for a generation after Gentile's death. And it is quite conceivable that painting in Umbria would have dribbled on in a failing, sickly stream, but for the providential aid suddenly sent from Florence. Not her greatest son did she speed thither, nor even one among her greatest. Benozzo Gozzoli came,—like many a Roman proconsul, second- or third-rate at home, yet a refulgent source of light and life in the distant British or Dacian province. And Benozzo not only woke to activity whatever latent talent there was in Umbria, not only furnished this talent with models to form itself upon, but, best of all, taught the Umbrians to look to Florence for instruction and enlightenment.

By far the most gifted of these native talents stung to consciousness by Benozzo was Lorenzo of Viterbo, who perished in his prime, leaving great paintings to his little town. There you may see a chapel frescoed by him—exuberant, full of splendid failure, more splendid promise, and great achievement withal. Seldom shall you witness a more spacious ceremony than his " Marriage of the Virgin," festive yet stately, filled with majestic men, staid matrons, and proud, life-enjoying youth—these, fitter suitors of Penelope than of the Galilean maiden.

Very different indeed was Niccolò da Foligno, in some respects the founder of the school in the narrower sense known as Umbrian—really the school of Perugia and its vale, —and certainly the first painter in whom the emotional, now passionate and violent, now mystic and ecstatic, temperament of St. Francis' countrymen was fully revealed. Regarded merely as an Illustrator, Niccolò ranks high. With a sincerity convincing beyond question,

he expresses the frantic grief of the believer
who has dwelt upon Christ's passion until he
himself almost feels the stigmata, brooded over
Mary's sorrow until he also is pierced with the
seven wounds of her anguish. Niccolò feels
penetratingly, expresses his wailful yearnings
unhushed, and makes no compromises. The
result is that, with the precisely identical purpose of the later Bolognese, he holds our attention, even gives us a certain pungent dolorous
pleasure, while we turn away from Guido Reni
with disgust unspeakable. These later painters
coquette in most unseemly fashion with the
flesh and the devil, even while they crucify
Christ, or torture a virgin martyr. Niccolò is
single-minded. You may dislike him as you
dislike Calderon, but his power is undeniable,
and he also was an artist—for Niccolò was not
devoid of feeling for line and colour, not un-
studied in the art of rendering movement.

XI.

And at last we are at Perugia, the Umbrian
capital, the town destined to shelter that school
of painting which, of all, is at once the most

pleasing and the most famous, the school which culminated in Raphael, the most beloved name in art.

But despite its grand destiny, Perugia was not peculiarly gifted with artistic genius, or it would not have called on Boccatis of Camerino, on Fra Angelico, on Benozzo Gozzoli, on Piero dei Franceschi and Luca Signorelli to supply the pictures it needed. Nor could much have been augured from Perugia's first native painter of note. As an artist Bonfigli scarcely ranks as high as Niccolò da Foligno, his fellow-pupil under Benozzo Gozzoli. He was a much more dependent person, but being more imitative, with the models of Fra Angelico or Benozzo before him, he at times painted exquisite things, and by nature he was gifted with that sense of the charming wherewith Perugia was later to take the world captive. Some of the freshest and loveliest of all angel faces may be seen in Bonfigli's altar-pieces and standards. His colour has almost always that hint of gold which never fades from Umbrian art. But far was it from him to harbour a feeling, no matter how faint, for what in painting is more essential

than charming faces and pretty colour : and no
degenerate Sienese ever was more garrulous
and incompetent than Bonfigli when he attempted historical composition. Such a task
was not to be performed by Perugians before
further contact with Florence had given them
as much acquaintance at least with form and
movement as was just necessary.

Fiorenzo di Lorenzo was thrice dipped in
the vivifying stream of Florentine art. At the
dawn of his career, Benozzo had been his inspiration ; while yet a youth, he put himself to
school at Florence under Antonio Pollaiuolo,
the great artist in movement ; and before returning to his provincial home, he learned
many a secret from Luca Signorelli. Fresh
from these beneficent influences, Fiorenzo
painted a series of panels recounting certain
miracles of St. Bernardino, in which we are
kept spell-bound by a beauty, a charm, a grace
peculiarly Umbrian, manifested in forms expressive of a feeling for line and movement
almost Florentine. How fascinating are these
scenes with their refined Renaissance edifices,
their garlanded triumphal arches opening on

the high-skied Umbrian valley, their romantic
landscapes, their lovely women, and their still
lovelier youth,—tall, slender, golden-haired,
dainty—Shakespeare's heroines in disguise!
Scarcely less enchanting as Illustrations, or less
strenuous in line, are other works of Fiorenzo's
splendid dawn, such as the " Nativity " in the
gallery of Perugia, or the "Annunciation"
decorating the Portiuncula, the first haunt of
the blessed St. Francis. But the inexorable
dullness of provincial ideals soon began to
exert its force upon him ; and he could not
long resist it. Struggle resulted in caricature,
and it was only much later, spurred on by the
triumphs of his pupils, that he again got out of
himself a work of art—the " Epiphany " of the
Perugia gallery.

These pupils, whose triumphs were so great
that to this day their names are among the
most familiar in art, were Pintoricchio and
Perugino. At first there scarcely could have
existed that disparity between their talents
which became so manifest later. Starting
nearly on a level, Perugino for many years was
ever to renew his strength by Antæan contact

with Florence; Pintoricchio never had such purification from provincial dry-rot, and the leaden cope of humdrum custom once settled upon him, the invigorating air of the outer world never touched him more.

But Pintoricchio's natural endowments were great, and his beginnings dazzling with promise. In the Sixtine Chapel he holds his own with the best of the *Quattrocento* painters, and may be looked at even alongside of Botticelli. Gentle feeling, lovely women and children, romantic landscape, clear arrangement, splendid portraiture, do their best to absorb and please us. As more serious tasks have been carefully avoided, there is nothing to suggest a higher plane of artistic activity. We lazily enjoy these frescoes as so much refined *genre*. And we shall find the same characteristics in most of his earlier works—all those in Rome which he executed with his own hand and without too much hurry. What lovely faces those of the angels in the Aracœli! What pretty women in the Borgia Apartments, or in S. Maria del Popolo! What splendid portraits, what romantic landscape everywhere! And, in addition to all this, how

much of that peculiarly Central Italian feeling
for arrangement and space which already we
found so noteworthy in the early Sienese,—a
feeling which we shall find more remarkable by
far in the Perugians. We shall look in vain
among earlier painters or other schools for a
scene more spacious within its limits, where
the figures are better placed, the architecture more nobly suggestive, where the landscape brings indoors more of its hypæthral
fragrance, than in Pintoricchio's lunette at S.
Maria del Popolo representing St. Jerome
preaching. Vainer still would be a search for
the setting of a ceremony more ample and gracious than the Aracœli " Funeral of St. Bernardino "—a city square, more noble, where one
would breathe more freely.

But if mere prettiness pleased so well, why
then, the more pretty faces, the more splendid
costumes, and romantic surroundings per square
foot, the better! And so Pintoricchio, never pos-
sessing much feeling for form or movement, now,
under the pressure of favour and popularity,
forgot their very existence, and tended to make
of his work an *olla podrida* rich and savoury,

but more welcome to provincial palates than to the few *gourmets*. And when such an opulent and luxurious half-barbarian as Pope Alexander VI. was his employer, then no spice nor condiment nor seasoning was spared, and a more gorgeously barbaric blaze of embossed gold and priceless ultramarine than in the Borgia Apartments you shall not soon see again!

As a painter, we could now leave Pintoricchio to the contempt he deserves. His later work, seriously considered, is all tinsel and costume-painting, a reversion to the worst Umbrian art of the beginning of the century—and, writing this, I do not forget the famous frescoes in the Libreria del Duomo at Siena. These frescoes, recounting the life and adventures of the great journalist and diplomat, afterwards Pope Pius II., bring me to the one further point I wish to make. As figure-painting, they scarcely could be worse. Not a creature stands on his feet, not a body exists; even the beauty of his women's faces has, through carelessness and thoughtless, constant repetition, become soured; as colour, these frescoes could hardly be gaudier or cheaper. And yet they have an undeniable charm. Bad as they are in every other way, they are almost perfect as architectonic decoration. Pintoricchio had been given an oblong room of no extraordinary dimensions ; but what did he not make of it ! Under a ceiling daintily enamelled with cunningly set-in panels of painting, grand arches open spaciously on romantic landscapes. You have a feeling of being under shelter, surrounded by all the splendour that wealth and art can contrive, yet in the open air—and that open air not boundless, raw, but measured off, its immensity made manifest by the arches which frame it, made commensurate with your own inborn feeling for roominess, but improved upon, extended, and harmonised, until you feel that there at last you can breathe so that mere breathing shall be music. Now it happens that certain processions, certain ceremonies, rather motley, not over-impressive, are going on in this enchanted out-of-doors. But you are so attuned that either you notice nothing unpleasant at all, or you take it as you would a passing band of music on a spring morning when your own pulses are dancing.

The last word, then, about Pintoricchio is that he was a great space-composer, even here not the equal of Perugino, and not to be admitted to the inner sanctuary where Raphael reigns supreme, yet great enough to retain in his worst daubs so much of this rare, tonic quality that, if you are not over-subtle in the analysis of your enjoyment, you will be ready to swear that these daubs are not daubs but most precious pictures.

XII.

And if space-composition could do so much for Pintoricchio, how much more could it accomplish for Perugino or Raphael, who possessed far greater dominion over it ! In them it was all clear gain, for, slight though their mastery over the most essential qualities in the figure arts, they took good care not to advertise their failings, and seldom do they offend by attempts too ambitious for their powers. Yet, aside from their greatness, particularly Raphael's, as Illustrators, their only conspicuous merit as artists was in space-composition, in which art Perugino surpassed all who ever came before him, and indeed all who came after him, excepting, however, his own pupil, Raphael, by whom even he was left far behind.

But what is this unheard-of art of space-composition? To begin with, it is not at all a synonym for " composition " as ordinarily used, a word by which, I take it, we mean such an arrangement of objects within a given area as will satisfy our feelings for symmetry, harmony, compactness, and clearness. But all this arrangement is with reference to a flat surface, and extensions up and down, to right and left of an ideal centre—not inwards,—and we already have met with a perfect example of this art in Duccio's " Incredulity of Thomas." Now space-composition differs from ordinary composition in the first place most obviously in that it is not an arrangement to be judged as extending only laterally, or up and down on a flat surface, but as extending inwards in depth as well. It is composition in three dimensions, and not in two, in the cube, not merely on the surface. And, though less obviously, space-composition differs even more widely from ordinary composition in its effect. The latter, reduced to its

elements, plays only on our feeling for pattern
—itself a compound of direct optical sensations
and their mental consequences, of faint impressions of balance, and fainter ideated movements.
Space-composition is much more potent. Pro-
ducing as it does immediate effects—how and
why cannot here be discussed—on the vaso-
motor system, with every change of space we
suffer on the instant a change in our circula-
tion and our breathing—a change which we become aware of as a feeling of heightened or
lowered vitality. The direct effect, then, of
space-composition is not only almost as powerful as that of music, but is brought about in
much the same way ; for, although many other
factors enter in to produce the impression made
by music, the body of its force grows out of the
revolutions it produces in the vaso-motor system. Hence the likeness so often felt, but, to
my knowledge at least, never explained, between
music and architecture,—the latter, in so far as
it is not merely superior carpentry, being essen-
tially a manifestation, the most specific and the
most powerful, of the art of space-composition.

With this last statement many will agree who

7

then will wonder how in painting space-composition can have a place, unless, indeed, it
reproduce architecture. But a painting that
represents architecture is intrinsically no more
of a space-composition than any other picture.
This art comes into existence only when we get
a sense of space not as a void, as something
merely negative, such as we customarily have,
but, on the contrary, as something very positive
and definite, able to confirm our consciousness
of being, to heighten our feeling of vitality.
Space-composition is the art which humanises
the void, making of it an enclosed Eden, a
domed mansion wherein our higher selves find
at last an abode, not only as comforting, as
measured to our every-day needs, as the homes
of the happier among us, but as transporting,
as exalting as are those things only which build
up the ideal life. Near as it is to music in the
form of great architecture, space-composition is
even more musical in painting; for here there
is less of the tyranny of mere masses of material,
and their inexorable suggestions of weight and
support; here there is more freedom, less is de-
determined for one, although nothing is left to

wayward fancy; and here, with this seeming greater freedom, many more instruments are playing to woo us away from our tight, painfully limited selves, and to dissolve us into the space presented, until at last we seem to become its indwelling, permeating spirit.

Space-composition in painting, then, is not the upstart rival of architecture, but its lovelier sister, an art capable of effects finer, more enchanting, more surely winning. And it produces its effects by totally different means. Architecture closes in and emprisons space, is largely an affair of interiors. Painted spacecomposition opens out the space it frames in, puts boundaries only ideal to the roof of heaven. All that it uses, whether the forms of the natural landscape, or of grand architecture, or even of the human figure, it reduces to be its ministrants in conveying a sense of untrammelled, but not chaotic spaciousness. In such pictures how freely one breathes,—as if a load had just been lifted from one's breast; how refreshed, how noble, how potent one feels; again, how soothed; and still again, how wafted forth to abodes of far-away bliss !

The feeling just described is one that, at happy moments, many of us have had in the presence of nature, and it is one that we expect, but too seldom get, from landscape-painting. Yet space-composition is as distinct from the art of landscape as it is from architecture. It can produce its effects with a grand city square (as indeed we have it in paintings by Piero dei Franceschi) no less, if not better, than with the lines of the hills; its triumphs do not depend on subtle modelling of the atmosphere, nor on elaborate study of light and shade. Nay, so little mere dexterity, skill, and science are required to succeed in this art, that, provided the artist have the feeling for it, and be brought up in a good tradition, even the poorest can attain to some success: and there scarcely can be found an Umbrian picture, wretched though it may be in all other respects, which does not win us by its pleasant sweep of space. And if our interest be really in the work of art—not in the artist, and his madness, triumph, or despair —we shall not despise space-composition because it requires less dexterity and skill than landscape-painting as now practised. Believe me, if you have no native feeling for space, not all the science, not all the labour in the world will give it you. And yet without this feeling there can be no perfect landscape. In spite of the exquisite modelling of Cézanne, who gives the sky its tactile values as perfectly as Michelangelo has given them to the human figure, in spite of all Monet's communication of the very pulse-beat of the sun's warmth over fields and trees, we are still waiting for a real art of landscape. And this will come only when some artist, modelling skies like Cézanne's, able to communicate light and heat as Monet does, will have a feeling for space rivalling Perugino's or even Raphael's. And because Poussin, Claude, and Turner have had much of this feeling, despite their inferiority in other respects to some of the artists of our own generation, they remain the greatest European landscape painters—for space-composition is the bone and marrow of the art of landscape.

XIII.

Now that we have some inkling of the resemblances and differences between space-composition on one side, and architecture and landscape-painting on the other; now that we understand why it has a distinct place among the arts, we shall be able to appreciate the real qualities of Perugino and Raphael, as otherwise we could not possibly have done. One point, however, still remains to be noted. It is this. Space-composition, as we agreed, woos us away from our tight, painfully limited selves, dissolves us into the space presented, until at last we seem to become its permeating, indwelling spirit. In other words, this wonderful art can take us away from ourselves and give us, while we are under its spell, the feeling of being identified with the universe, perhaps even of being the soul of the universe. The feeling may be so conscious that it remains an artistic sensation— the most artistic of all; or it may transport one into the raptures of mysticism; but for those of us who are neither idolaters nor suppliants, this sense of identification with the universe is of the very essence of the religious emotion—an emotion, by the way as independent of belief and conduct as love itself. And now mark whither we have come. The religious emotion—for

some of us entirely, for others at least in part—
is produced by a feeling of identification with the
universe ; this feeling, in its turn, can be created
by space-composition ; it follows then that this
art can directly communicate religious emotion
—or at least all the religious emotion that many
of us really have, good church-members though
we may be. And indeed I scarcely see by
what other means the religious emotion can be
directly communicated by painting—mark you,
I do not say represented.

If, then space-composition is the only art intrinsically religious, since the Perugian school
is the great mistress of this art, we see why the
paintings of Perugino and Raphael produce, as
no others, the religious emotion. And so strong
is it when produced, that the haunting quandary
of commonplace minds is how Perugino could
have painted pictures so profoundly religious
and yet have been an atheist and a villain.

If here it were our business to discuss the
relation of the work of art to the artist, it could
be pointed out that a villain and an atheist
might paint sweet, holy people because he preferred them in life, finding them easier victims,

lovely, tender, pure women, because they were a rarer or more fragile prey. Finding these people more convenient, he might even be crafty enough to do what he could to add to their number by painting pictures that would wake those who looked on them to a consciousness of preference for a life holy and refined. All this is a quite conceivable, but here at least an unnecessary, hypothesis. Perugino, as I have but now said, produces his religious effect by means of his space-composition. Of his figures we require no more than that they shall not disturb this feeling, and if we take them as we should, chiefly as architectonic members in the effect of space, they seldom or ever disturb us. Their stereotyped attitudes and expressions we should judge, not as if they were persons in a drama, but as so many columns or arches, of which we surely would not demand dramatic variety.

Not that Perugino was contemptible as a mere Illustrator. Far from it! He had a feeling for beauty in women, charm in young men, and dignity in the old, seldom surpassed before or since. Then there is a well ordered seemliness, a sanctuary aloofness in all his people which makes them things apart, untouched and pure. Great reserve also does much for him. Violent action he doubtless avoided because he felt himself unequal to the task—indeed, so little did he ever master movement that his figures when walking, dance on tiptoe, and on their feet they never stand; but he as carefully kept away from unseemly expression of emotion. How refreshingly quiet are his Crucifixions and Entombments! The still air is soundless, and the people wail no more; a sigh inaudible, a look of yearning, and that is all. How soothing must such paintings have been after the din and turmoil and slaughter of Perugia, the bloodiest town in Italy! Can it be wondered that men, women, and children ran to see them? Nor yet is life so free from sordid cares and meaningless broils that we can forego such balm for the soul as Perugino brings.

The space effect, however, plays so important a part in his compositions that it becomes difficult to say just how much of their quality is due to other factors. We shall be surer of our judgment if we look at one or two of

Perugino's portraits.   In young Messer Alessandro Braccesi we have the type so recurrent
in the pictures, and we see that it loses little of
its Peruginesque charm, although here there is
no transfiguring background.   And even in a
portrait where there is a most soothing special
accompaniment, the one, in the Uffizi, of Francesco dell' Opere, Perugino shows his great mastery over Illustration by presenting to us one
of the most ably interpreted, most firmly char-
acterised, most convincing faces in the whole
range of Renaissance art—so powerful a face
that all the poppy drowsiness of the landscape
cannot soften down its rigour.   And how little
of swooning sentimentality there really was in
his nature we may infer from that sternly mat-
ter-of-fact self-appreciation, his own portrait in
the Cambio at Perugia.

Remarkable, however, as are Perugino's qualities as an Illustrator, I doubt whether we should
rank him among the great artists for these
alone.   They are not sufficient—if, indeed, even
the very highest reaches of mere Illustration
ever are—to make up for a deficiency in feeling
either for form or movement, a deficiency not

so deplorable, thanks to his repeated contact
with Florence, as Pintoricchio's, yet sad enough.
But so potent was his charm as a space-composer that we never take his figures seriously as
figures—or, if we do, we are wrong; for to
quarrel with them is no wiser than to make ado
about silly words set to a solemn music. These
figures got worse and worse as he grew older,
and, finally, when art already was awhirl with
the revelation of Michelangelo, Perugino, alto-
gether retiring from the struggle to count among
artists, ceased visiting Florence, and lost what
sense he ever had possessed for the figure and
the nude. But his feeling for space he could
not lose; nay, it gained in strength when, no
longer wasting vitality on the effort of painting
the figure as for itself it should be painted—an
effort repugnant to his nature,—he gave loose
rein to his native impulse. He spent the last
years of his life wreathing the Umbrian hills
with his golden art, leaving on the walls of many
a wayside shrine skies and horizons ineffable.

And now let us look more closely at a few
of Perugino's compositions. One of his earliest
works is the fresco, in the Sixtine Chapel, of

"Christ Giving the Keys to Peter," a work in which he has given more attention to structure than you shall find him doing again. As if by miracle, several persons are standing on their feet. Note, however, that these are neither Christ nor the Apostles, whom doubtless Pietro was already painting by rote, but portraits of his own friends. And as if to explain the miracle, he has, on the extreme left, introduced himself standing by Luca Signorelli, from whom he then was drawing his inspiration. Yet you will not find even these persons life-enhancing by means of their tactile values or their movement. And throughout this fresco, Perugino's figures are no more attractive than Pintoricchio's, no better constructed than in the frescoes of those Florentine mediocrities, Cosimo Rosselli and Ghirlandaio, in movement contemptible beside Botticelli. And still among the paintings of the Sixtine Chapel Perugino's is certainly not the least agreeable. Nay, is there one more delightful? It is the golden, joyous colour, the fine rhythm of the groups, and above all the buoyant spaciousness of this fresco that

win and hold us. Our attention first falls on
the figures in the foreground, which measured
against the pavement cunningly tesselated for
the purpose, at once suggest a scale more
commensurate with the vastness of nature
than with the puniness of man. Nor do these
grand figures crowd the square. Far from it.
Spacious, roomy, pleasantly empty, it stretches
beyond them, inward and upward, over groups
of men, surely of the same breed, but made
small by the distance, until, just this side of
the horizon's edge, your eye rests on a temple
with soaring cupola and airy porticoes, the
whole so proportioned to the figures in the
foreground, so harmonised with the perspective of the pavement, that you get the feeling
of being under a celestial dome, not shut in
but open and free in the vastness of the space.
The effect of the whole is perfectly determined
both by the temple, through which runs the
axis of this ideal hemisphere, and by the foreground, which suggests its circumference. And
taking it as a sphere, you are compelled to
feel as much space above and beyond the dome
as there is between it and yourself.

We have no time to dwell at this length on
Perugino's other paintings.   But a few must not
pass unmentioned.   How cool in its warmth
is the effect of the Albani Polyptych, with its
space continuous through the various panels,
felt though beautiful arches, stretching to
enchanted distances, evoking freshness and
fragrance, bringing back to you those rare
moments when, new to life, in the early hour
of a summer morning, for an instant you tasted
of Paradise.   Of Perugino's pictures in the
Louvre alone, four have this golden, dreamy
summeriness : the idyll, more than Theocritan,
of " Apollo and Marsyas "; the dainty small
" St. Sebastian," of Pietro's later years ; and
two earlier works : the round containing the
Madonna with guardian Saints and Angels, all
dipped in the colour of heaven, dreaming away
in bliss the glowing summer afternoon ; and,
finally, the large " St. Sebastian," enframed
under an arch which opens out on Eden, and
measuring, not as in *plein-air* painting, a mite
against infinity, but as man should in Eden,
dominant and towering high over the horizon.
It is this exaltation of the human being over

the landscape that not only justifies but renders great, paintings otherwise so feeble as the frescoes in the Cambio of Perugia—even the feeblest of them, the one where you see two lovely women unrecognisable, save for their symbols, as "Strength of Will" and "Temperance," and on the ground below them dreamy, lackadaisical, pretty knights and captains, still less recognisable as renowned exemplifiers of these virtues, yet grand and columnar in their relation to the vastness of the landscape. Far better, despite its somewhat gaunt blues, is the Triptych of the National Gallery, mellow in its gold, with the adoring Virgin supereminent over nature, and the singing Angels turning the sky they float in to the apse of some aërial cathedral. Without the transmuting power of the spacious pavilion opening out on the Umbrian vale, what would be the value of the Munich panel representing the "Virgin Appearing to St. Bernard"? What but the uplifting skies and soothing distances draws your steps at Florence to the "Crucifixion" in S. Maria Maddalena de' Pazzi?

XIV.

And now we are face to face with the most famous and most beloved name in modern art —Raphael Sanzio.   There have been in the last five centuries artists of far greater genius. Michelangelo was grander and more powerful, Leonardo at once more profound and more refined.   In Raphael you never get the sweet world's taste as in Giorgione, nor its full pride and splendour as in Titian and Veronese.   And I am calling up only Italian names—how many others, if we chose to cross the Alps !—and it is only as Illustrator that he rivals these : for in the more essential matters of figure-painting Raphael is not for a moment to be ranked on a level with the great Florentines ; nor does he, like the Venetians, indelibly dye the world with resplendent colour.   If you measure him with the standards that you would apply to artists like Pollaiuolo or Degas, you will soon condemn him to the radiant limbo of heavily gilt mediocrities ;   for movement and form were to his temperament, if not to his mind, as repugnant as ever they were to his patri-

archal precursor, Duccio. Sift the legions of
drawings ascribed to him until you have reduced their number to the few unmistakably his.
Would you then venture to place even these
few among the works of the greatest draughts-
men? Or look at his " Entombment," the only
composition which he attempted to treat entirely as every serious figure-painting should
be treated, for the tactile values and the movement that it may be made to impart. You see
that the poor creature, most docile and patient,
had toiled and sweated to achieve what his
head understood but his heart felt not—direct
communications of force. The result is one of
the most uncouth "academies" that may be
seen, at least outside of that charnel-house of
prize pictures, the diploma gallery of the École
des Beaux Arts at Paris.

Ever ready to learn, Raphael passed from influence to influence. At whose feet did he not sit?
Timoteo Viti's, Perugino's, and Pintoricchio's,
Michelangelo's, Leonardo's, and Fra Bartolommeo's, and finally, Sebastian del Piombo's. From
the last named, Sanzio, then already at the very
height of his career and triumph, humbly

endeavoured to acquire those potent secrets of magical colour which even a second-rate Venetian could teach him. And although he learned his lesson well, for in this the Umbrians ever had been distant cousins, as it were, of the Venetians, yet twice only did he attain to signal achievement in colour : the fresco, so splendid as mere painting, which represents the " Miracle of Bolsena," and that exquisite study in grey, the " Portrait of Baldassare Castiglione." But what are these beside the mural paintings of Veronese, or the portraits of Titian ? At his rarest best Raphael, as a master of colour, never went beyond Sebastiano.

Whether then we are on the outlook for eminent mastery over form and movement, or for great qualities of colour and mere painting, Raphael will certainly disappoint us. But he has other claims on our attention—he was endowed with a visual imagination which has never even been rivalled for range, sweep, and sanity. When it has been surpassed, it has been at single points and by artists of more concentrated genius. Thus gifted, and coming at a time when form had, for its own sake, been recovered

by the Naturalists and the essential artists,
when the visual imagery, of at least the Italian
world, had already suffered along certain lines,
the transformation from the Mediæval into
what ever since has been for all of us the mod'
ern, when the ideals of the Renaissance were
for an ineffable instant standing complete,
Raphael, filtering and rendering lucid and pure
all that had passed through him to make him
what he was, set himself the task of dowering
the modern world with the images that to this
day, despite the turbulent rebellion and morose
secession of recent years, embody for the great
number of cultivated men their spiritual ideals
and their spiritual aspirations. "*Belle comme une
madonne de Raphael*" is, among the most artistic people in Europe, still the highest praise that
can be given to female beauty. And, in sooth,
where shall one find greater purity, more utter
loveliness than in his "Granduca Madonna," or a
sublimer apparition of woman than appeared to
St. Sixtus? Who, as a boy reading his Homer,
his Virgil, or his Ovid, and dreaming dreams
and seeing visions, but has found them realised
a thousand fold in the "Parnassus"! Who has

ever had an ideal of intellectual converse in
noble surroundings but has looked with yearning at the "Disputa" and the "School of
Athens"!   Has Galatea ever haunted you?
Tell me, has she not imparted a thousand times
more life and freedom and freshness since you
have seen her painted by Raphael in the midst
of her Tritons and Sea-Nymphs? Antiquity
itself has, in the figure-arts, left no embodiment
so exultingly complete of its own finest imagin-
ings.

We go to Raphael for the beautiful vesture
he has given to the Antiquity of our yearnings;
and as long as the world of the Greeks and
Romans remains for us what I fervently pray it
may continue to be, not only a mere fact, but a
longing and a desire, for such a time shall we,
as we read the Greek and Latin poets, accom-
pany them with an imagery either Raphael's
own, or based on his; so long shall we see their
world as Raphael saw it—a world where the
bird of morning never ceased to sing.

What wonder then that Raphael became on
the instant, and has ever remained, the most
beloved of artists! A world which owed all

that was noblest and best in it to classical culture, found at last its artist, the Illustrator who,
embodying Antiquity in a form surpassing its
own highest conceptions, satisfied at last its
noblest longings. Raphael, we may say, was
the master artist of the Humanists, and the
artist of people nurtured on the Classics he
remains.

But there is in our civilisation another element which, though it is certainly much less
important in our conscious intellectual life,
and of much less interest to the pictorial imagination, is said, nevertheless, to be morally superior and poetically grander—all the Hebraic
element, I mean, that has come to us from the
Old and New Testaments. Sanzio here, also,
performed a task by which we have benefited
ever since, for, imperturbably Hellenic in spirit,
he has given an Hellenic garb to the Hebraic
universe. In pictures which he either executed
or superintended, or at least inspired, Raphael
has completely illustrated both the Old and New
Testaments; and such has been the spell of
these Illustrations that they have trickled down
to the lowest strata of society, and it will take

not one but ten thousand M. Tissots to win even the populace away from them. And this imagery, in which Raphael has clothed the Hebrew world for us, is no more Hebraic than that of Virgil, singing the new order of things when the lion shall lie down with the lamb. Raphael has brought about the extraordinary result that when we read even the Hebrew classics, we read them with an accompaniment of Hellenic imagery. What a power he has been in modern culture, Hellenising the only force that could have thwarted it! If you would have examples in proof of what I have been saying, look at the *Loggia*, look at the cartoons for the tapestries, look at Marcantonio's engravings, but look, above all, in the Pitti at the " Vision of Ezechiel." Is it thus that Jehovah revealed himself to his prophets? Is it not rather Zeus appearing to a Sophocles?

Raphael has enshrined all the noble tenderness and human sublimity of Christianity, all the glamour and edifying beauty of the antique world, in forms so radiant that we ever return to them to renew our inspiration. But has he not also given us our ideals of beauty? The

Florentines were too great as figure-artists, the
Venetians as masters of colour and paint, to
care much for that which in Art, as distin-
guished from Illustration, is so unimportant as
what in life we call beauty. The " beautiful
woman," is apt to be what the real artist con-
siders a bad subject—one in the painting of
which it is exceedingly difficult, if at all possible,
to present form or line. Such a woman, delightful though she may be in life, and ethically
and socially perhaps the most desirable type,
is apt to become in art a vulgar chromo. Many
efforts have been made in our times, by artists
who were mere Illustrators—or at least have
had influence as such only,—to change the ideal ;
but the fatalistic and ailing woman they tried
to make popular, though more attractive to
tastes bored with health and lovableness, is
not in itself any more artistic than the other.
So the type of beauty to which our eyes and
desire still return is Raphael's—the type which
for four hundred years has fascinated Europe.
Not artist enough to be able to do without
beauty, and the heir of the Sienese feelings for
loveliness, too powerfully controlled by Floren-

tine ideals not to be guided somewhat by their restraining and purifying art, Sanzio produced a type, the composite of Ferrarese, Central Italian and Florentine conceptions of female beauty, which, as no other, has struck the happy mean between the instinctive demands of life and the more conscious requirements of art. And he was almost as successful in his types of youth or age—indeed, none but Leonardo ever conceived any lovelier or more dignified. Only for manhood was Raphael perhaps too feeble—and yet, I am not sure.

A surprise awaits us. This painter whose temperament we fancy to have been somewhat languid, who presented ideals Hesperidean, idyllic, Virgilian, could, when he chose, be not only grand in his conceptions—that we know already,—but severe, impassive, and free from any aim save that of interpreting the object before him. And Raphael's portraits, in truth, have no superiors as faithful renderings of soul and body. They are truthful even to literal veracity, perceived in piercing light, yet reconstructed with an energy of intellectual and artistic fusion that places them among the

constellations. Need we cite instances? Bear
in mind the various portraits in the *Stanze* of
Julius II.; the cruel refinement of the Madrid
bust of a young Cardinal; the genial faces of
Navagero and Beazzano; the brutish greasiness
of Leo X., nevertheless not wholly repellent;
and, best of all, the majestic portrait of a young
Roman matron—such as Cornelia must have
looked—known in the Pitti as "La Donna
Velata."

XV.

But was this, then, all Raphael's merit—that
he was a lovable Illustrator, the most lovable
that we have ever had? With the vanishing
of that world, offspring of Antiquity and the
Renaissance, we now live in; with the breaking
of that infinite chain of associations each link
of which has the power to make us throb with
joy;—if the ochlocracy prevail in our midst,
not restrained as during the French Revolution
by sublime catch-words, but at last persuaded
that man lives on bread alone; or, worse fate,
if, in the more than thrice millennial but still
undecided duel between Europe and Asia,

little Europe finally succumb to the barbarians;
then, should another culture ever upspring,
and in it people capable of appreciating art,
what (if by miracle his work survived) would
they find in Raphael? As an Illustrator he
would mean at the utmost no more to them
than, as mere Illustrators, the great artists of
China and Japan mean to us. He would not
embody their ideals nor express their aspirations, nor be conjuring up to their minds
subtly appreciative sensations, feelings, and
dreams, emprisoned, since the glowing years
of childhood, in the limbo of their unconscious selves, and needing the artist to fetch
them out to the light. They could enjoy him,
only as we who know nothing or next to nothing of the myths, poetry, or history of China
and Japan, yet take pleasure in the art of those
countries—as pure Art, independent of all
accidents and all circumstances, confined to
the divine task of heightening our vital and
mental processes. And as pure Art, what
supreme distinction would they discover in
Raphael? Such as were wise enough to continue their quest, although they found him

lacking in the qualities essential to the figure-arts, lacking also in the gifts which make the great craftsman, would end by seeing that he, Raphael Sanzio, was the greatest master of Composition—whether considered as arrangement or as space—that Europe down to the end of the nineteenth century had ever produced.

What space-composition is, we already know, and here we need not discuss it again. It will suffice to examine a few of Raphael's masterpieces, as before we looked at certain of Perugino's. The earliest, and perhaps loveliest revelation of Raphael's gift we shall find in his "Sposalizio." In essentials it is, as a space-composition, but a variation on the fresco of Perugino that we studied in the Sixtine Chapel; the same grouping in the foreground, the same middle distance, the same closing of the horizon with a domed temple. The elements and the principle remain the same, but the indwelling spirit is not the same. Subtler feeling for space, greater refinement, even a certain daintiness, give this "Sposalizio" a fragrance, a freshness that are not in Perugino's fresco. In presence of young Sanzio's picture you feel a poignant thrill of transfiguring sensation, as if, on a morning early, the air cool and dustless, you suddenly found yourself in presence of a fairer world, where lovely people were taking part in a gracious ceremony, while beyond them stretched harmonious distances line on line to the horizon's edge.

The space effect of Perugino's great fresco we compared to a celestial dome; but there perhaps it will escape you if you do not look carefully. Raphael, perchance more aware of just what he was seeking, produces a similar effect, but unmistakable, and grander. Look in the *Stanze* at that majestic theophany known as the "Disputa." On the top of Olympus the gods and heroes are assembled in council. They are so arranged that the most obvious architecture could not better indicate the depth and roundness of a dome; but no architectural dome could so well convey a sense of the vastness yet commensurability, nay, shall we not say of the companionship of space. How much greater, how much purer than one's ordinary self—how transfigured one feels here!

The forms in the "Disputa" are noble in intention, as they always are in Raphael's best work. But think away the spaciousness of their surroundings. What has become of the solemn dignity, the glory that radiated from them? It has gone like divinity from a god. And the other fresco, the "School of Athens," would suffer still more from such treatment. We have a cartoon of this subject with the figures only, and we have Raphael's painting. How ordinary and second-rate are the mere figures; how transformed when seen against those sublime arches, almost the grandest ever conceived! And not only are the figures ennobled, but yourself. How like a demigod you feel here in this lighter, purer air!

And what decorations for a small room! Into a room of dimensions almost mean and far from tempting to the decorator, the "Disputa" and the "School of Athens," the "Parnassus" and the pure space occupied by "Justice," bring all the out-of-doors of some Eden, where man has no sordid cares, no struggles, where thought and art are his only occupations.

For Raphael was not only the greatest Space-Composer that we have ever had, but the greatest master of Composition in the more usual sense of grouping and arrangement. Before we leave the *Stanza della Segnatura*, look again at the " Disputa." Note the balance of the masses about the Host, note the flow towards it of all the lines. Upon it your eye must rest. Or in the " School of Athens " see how everything converges towards Plato and Aristotle, the effect further enhanced by the enframing distant arch against which they stand. It is the effect that we found in Duccio's "Incredulity of Thomas," but here on a scale almost cosmic. In the ceiling of the same *Stanza* is a " Judgment of Solomon." Have you ever seen a flat space better filled, a clearer arrangement and better balance of masses? A kindred effect you may see in the Farnesina, where concave spherical triangles are so admirably filled with paintings of the various adventures of Psyche, that you think of them as openings revealing scenes that are passing, never as awkward spaces almost hopelessly difficult to deal with.

But hard as it may be to fill spaces like these,

it is yet no task beside the difficulty of treating one group, perhaps one figure only, so that, perfectly dominating the space at command, it shall not become too abstract and schematic and fixed, but shall suggest freedom, evoke an environment of air and sunshine. When looking at the "Granduca Madonna," has it ever occurred to you to note that the whole of her figure was not there? So perfect is the arrangement that the attention is entirely absorbed by the grouping of the heads, the balance of the Virgin's draped arm and the Child's body. You are not allowed to ask yourself how the figure ends. And observe how it holds its own, easily poised, in the panel which is just large enough to contain it without crowding, without suggesting room for aught beside.

But great as is the pleasure in a single group perfectly filling a mere panel, it is far greater when a group dominates a landscape. Raphael tried several times to obtain this effect—as in the "Madonna del Cardellino," or the "Madonna del Prato," but he attained to supreme success once only—in the "*Belle*

Jardinière." Here you have the full negation
of the *plein-air* treatment of the figure. The
Madonna is under a domed sky, and she fills it
completely, as subtly as in the Granduca panel,
but here it is the whole out-of-doors, the universe, and a human being supereminent over
it. What a scale is suggested! Surely the
spiritual relation between man and his environment is here given in the only way that man—
unless he become barbarised by decay, or non-
humanised by science—will ever feel it. And
not what man knows but what man feels, concerns art. All else is science.

XVI.

To resume, Raphael was not an artist in the
sense that Michelangelo, Leonardo, Velasquez,
or even Rembrandt was. He was a great Illustrator and a great Space-Composer. But the
success he attained was his ruin; for, obliged
in the later years of his brief life, to work
hastily, superintending a horde of assistants,
seldom with leisure for thought, he felt too
pressed to work out his effects either as Illustration or as Space-Composition; so that most

of his later work lacks the qualities of either of
these arts, over which he was the natural master.

And if this were so with him, how much
worse with his pupils, his executants, brought
up on hurry and turmoil, none of whom had
talents either as Illustrators or as Space-Com-
posers! And in truth what more unpalatable
than their work? They have none of that feeling for space which pleases even in the worst
immediate followers of Perugino; none of that
pleasant colour which attracts us to even the
meanest Venetian. No wonder that we have
given over Giulio Romano, Pierino del Vaga,
Giovan Franceschi Penni, Michelangelo Cara-
vaggio, and their ignoble fellows to oblivion. It
is all they deserve.

But let not these names come to our minds
when we think of the artists of Central Italy,
but the names of the splendid cohort of great
Illustrators, great Figure-Artists, great Space-
Composers, led by the bright genius of Duccio
and Simone Martini, of Piero dei Franceschi and
Signorelli, of Perugino and Raphael.

9

INDEX TO THE WORKS OF THE PRINCI-
PAL CENTRAL ITALIAN PAINTERS.

NOTE.

The following lists make no claim to absolute completeness, but no genuine work by the painters mentioned, found in the better known public or private collections, has been omitted. With the exception of three or four pictures, which he knows only in the photographs, the author has seen and carefully studied every picture indicated, and is alone responsible for the attributions, although he is happy to acknowledge his indebtedness to the writings of Signor Cavalcaselle, of the late Giovanni Morelli, of Signor Gustavo Frizzoni, and of Dr. J. P. Richter.

Public galleries are mentioned first, then private collections, and churches last. The principal public gallery is always understood after the simple mention of a city or town. Thus, Paris means Paris, Louvre, London means London, National Gallery, etc.

An interrogation point after the title of a picture indicates that its attribution to the given painter is doubtful. Distinctly early or late works are marked E. or L.

It need scarcely be said that the attributions here given are not based on official catalogues, and are often at variance with them.

ALUNNO *see* NICCOLÒ.

MATTEO BALDUCCI.

Sienese. Active first quarter of sixteenth century. Pupil probably of Fungai ; assistant and imitator of Pintoricchio.

Bergamo. MORELLI, 46. Flight of Clelia.

Berlin. 120. Madonna and two Saints.

HERR KAUFMANN. Madonna.

Bourges. Madonna and Infant John.

Buda-Pesth. 35. Madonna and Infant John. (?)

Cologne. 778, 779. Two female Saints.

Dresden. 36. St. Crispin.

Gubbio. MUNICIPIO. Bacchanal.

London. LORD CRAWFORD. Diana and Actæon.

Milan. SIGNOR CRESPI. St. Catherine receiving Stigmata.

Montpellier. 573. St. Christopher. (?)

Oxford. CHRIST CHURCH, 21. Madonna with two female Saints and two Angels.

Paris. 1571. Judgment of Solomon.

1572. Judgment of Daniel.

M. RAVAISSON. Apollo and Admetus.

Richmond. SIR F. COOK. St. John. St. Jerome.

Rome. VATICAN, MUSEO CRISTIANO, CASE T, IV. Triptych : Assumption of Virgin with SS. Jerome and Gregory, 1497. (?)

Rouen. 55. Sacrifice to Vesta.

Siena. SALA VIII, 21. Angel.

34. Madonna with SS. Francis and Catherine.

SALA IX, 2. St. Jerome and the Magdalen.

10. Justice.

11. Strength.

14. Madonna with SS. Jerome and Francis.

Siena (*Con.*). 15. Faith.

  17. Madonna with SS. Jerome and Bartholo-
       mew.

  19. Charity.

  25. *Predella* in three compartments.

  26. Nativity.

  28. Nativity.

  37. SS. Agnes and Francis.

OPERA DEL DUOMO, 14. St. Antony of Padua.

PALAZZO SARACINI. Cassone : Dream of Hercules.

  Tondo : Venus and Cupid.

  Tondo : Putto in Landscape.

DUOMO, LIBRERIA. Frescoes : Mythological and
  Allegorical scenes on ceiling ; Shields over
  windows ; and monochromes in pilasters.

PAVEMENT (from design) : Allegory of For-
  tune, 1505.

(All these under direct inspiration of Pintoricchio.)

RICOVERO (CAMPANSI), CLOISTER. Fresco : Assumption of Virgin (God, Prophets and Angels by Pietro di Domenico).

S. SPIRITO, IST ALTAR L. Madonna in Glory
  with Saints.

BARTOLI *see* TADDEO.

BARTOLO *see* DOMENICO.

DOMENICO BECCAFUMI.*

Sienese. 1485–1551. Pupil of Pacchiarotto ; influenced by
Sodoma and Fra Bartolommeo.

* More interesting works only.

Altenburg.	Tondo : Holy Family and Infant John.
Berlin.	HERR WESENDONCK, 5. Quintus Curtius.
Florence.	PITTI. 259. Holy Family.
	UFFIZI, 189. Holy Family.
	PALAZZO TORRIGIANI. Holy Family.
Hamburg.	CONSUL WEBER, 112. Holy Family and Saints.
London.	1430. Story of Esther.
	MR. R. BENSON. Flight of Clelia.
	HERTFORD HOUSE. Judith.
Lucca.	SALA I, 60. Continence of Scipio.
Munich.	1076. Holy Family.
Panshauger.	LORD COWPER. Holy Family.
Pisa.	DUOMO, CHOIR. The Four Evangelists, 1539.
	Moses and the Tablets of the Law, 1538.
	Moses and the Children of Korah, 1538.
Rome.	DORIA, 276. St. Jerome.
Siena.	SALA VIII, 17. Baptism.
	SALA X, 6. Nativity.
	10. Trinity and four Siants, 1512.
	19–21. Story of St. Catherine.
	22. St. Catherine receiving the Stigmata.
	25. Fall of Lucifer.
	28. Christ in Limbo.
	OPERA DEL DUOMO. St. Paul enthroned.
	PALAZZO PUBBLICO, UPPER HALL. Ceiling Frescoes : 1529–1535.
	PALAZZO BINDI–SERGARDI. Continence of Scipio, and other Ceiling Frescoes.
	PALAZZO SARACINI. Madonna.
	Large Altar-piece : Madonna with SS. Peter and Paul.
	Lucretia.
	Putti upholding a gold Globe.
	Cassone : Rape of Sabines.
	DUOMO, CHOIR. Frescoes (ruined), 1544.
	CARMINE, 5TH ALTAR L. St. Michael.

Siena (*Con.*). S. Martino, 3rd Altar L.   Nativity.

Oratorio di S. Bernardino.   Altar-piece :
Madonna with six Saints, 1537.

Frescoes : Sposalizio ; Death of Virgin, 1518.

Ricovero (Campansi), 1st Floor. Fresco : Madonna with the Magdalen and SS. Anne and
Ursula.

Spedale, Entrance Hall. Fresco : Visitation,
1512.

S. Spirito, Cloister. Coronation.

Strassburg. Bust of Man.

Venice.   Seminario. Penelope.

BENVENUTO DI GIOVANNI.

Sienese. 1436–1518 (?). Pupil of Vecchietta. Influenced by
Francesco di Giorgio.

Asciano.   S. Sebastiano.   Fresco.   Assumption and
Saints.

Buda-Pesth. 24. Nativity.

42. Madonna and two Angels.

Florence.   Sig. Bardini. Nativity. Fresco : St. Benedict.

Marchese Pio Strozzi. Polyptych. Scenes
from Passion.

Liverpool. 20.   St. Bernardino preaching.(?)

21.   Birth of John.

London.   909.   Triptych : Madonna and two Saints.

Lord Ashburnham. Madonna and two Angels
with Flowers.

Mr. G. Salting. Madonna.

New Haven, U. S. A. Jarves Collection. 59. Madonna and two Angels.

71. Love bound by Maidens (a Salver).

Paris.   M. Chabrières Arlès. Madonna.

Perugia. Sala IV, 21. Pietà.

Richmond. SIR F. COOK. Four Predelle with Scenes from the Passion.

Profile of a Lady.

Rome. CORSINI. 705. Crucifixion.

VATICAN, MUSEO CRISTIANO, CASE O, XIV. Franciscan tried by Fire.

XV. Duel and Reconciliation.

Siena. SALA X, 37. Ascension, 1491.

38. Predella of No. 39, in four Compartments.

39. Triptych: Madonna and Saints, 1475.

ARCHIVIO. Book covers: Allegory of Peace and War, 1468;

Liberty Enthroned, 1474; Four Companies united in Duomo receiving Keys, 1483.

PALAZZO PALMIERI-NUTI. Four small busts of Saints.

ABBAZIA DI S. EUGENIO. Frescoes: R. WALL. Resurrection;

L. WALL. Crucifixion.

CONFRATERNITÀ DELLA MADONNA SOTTO LE VOLTE DELL' OSPEDALE. St. Catherine bringing back Pope Gregory from Avignon, 1501.

DUOMO, PAVEMENT (from a design). Tiburtine Sibyl, 1483.

RICOVERO (Campansi) First Floor. Fresco: " Noli me Tangere."

S. DOMENICO. L. Transept, 2d Chapel. Madonna and Saints. Pietà (in Lunette), 1483.

S. SEBASTIANO IN VALLE PIATTA. Sacristy. Madonna with SS. James and Jerome.

Volterra. PALAZZO DEI PRIORI. Annunciation and Saints, 1466.

DUOMO. Nativity and Predelle, 1466.

GIOVANNI BATTISTA BERTUCCI.

Worked 1503–1516. Influenced by Perugino, Pintoricchio, Costa, and Francia.

Berlin. 132. Adoration of Magi.

Buda-Pesth. 60. Madonna and St. Catherine.

Faenza. Madonna and four Saints, 1511.
Altar-piece in four Compartments, 1506.
Nativity.
Adoration of Magi.
Magdalen.
Baptist.
" Noli me Tangere."
SIGNOR VINCENZO GUIDI. Coronation (lunette).
The Young Baptist.
God, the Father, and two Cherubs.

Florence. MARCHESE IPPOLITO GINORI. Two Mythological Scenes.

London. 282. Glorification of Virgin.
646. St. Catherine.
647. St. Ursula.
1051. Incredulity of Thomas.
LORD ALDENHAM. St. John the Evangelist.

Paris. MME. Édouard Andrè. Narcissus.

Scotland. LINLATHEN, COL. ERSKINE. Madonna and Infant John.
NEW BATTLE, MARQUIS OF LOTHIAN. SS. Peter and Stephen.

GIOVANNI BOCCATIS.

Umbrian. Active 1435 (?)–1460 (?). Pupil of Lorenzo di San Severino, the Elder ; influenced by Pier dei Franceschi.

Frankfort a/M. 2. Coronation of Virgin.
London. Mr. C. Butler. Madonna.
Milan. Poldi-Pezzoli, 115. Madonna and Angels.
Perugia. Sala VI, 16. Madonna and Angels.
    17. Madonna and Angels.
    18. Madonna of Mercy.
    19. Madonna and Angels, Doctors of the Church and Saints, 1447.
    20. Predella to above : Scenes from Passion, and two Saints.

BENEDETTO BONFIGLI.

Umbrian. About 1425–1496. Pupil perhaps of Boccatis ; developed under influence of Fra Angelico and Benozzo Gozzoli.

Berlin. 137A. Madonna with Mary and Martha. E.
Empoli. Opera del Duomo. 22. Madonna with SS. Sebastian, Barbara, Antony Abbot, and Matthew.
London. Mr. Henry Wagner. Madonna surrounded by Angels holding lilies and making music. E.
Perugia. Sala I, 7. Ecce Homo.
    Sala II. Frescoes : Stories of St. Louis of Toulouse and St. Ercolano. Begun 1454 ; not quite finished when he died.
    Sala V, 35. Madonna and Angels.(?) E.
    Sala VI, 7. Annunciation and St. Luke.
        9. Predelle : Baptism ; Crucifixion ; Miracles of St. Nicholas of Bari.
        10. Adoration of Magi.
        11. SS. Paul and Peter Martyr (assisted by Caporali).

Perugia (*Con.*). 12. Madonna (from an Annunciation) (assisted by Caporali).

        13. Madonna and music-making Angels (assisted by Caporali).

        14. SS. Peter and Catherine (assisted by Caporali).

        15. The Angel Gabriel (assisted by Caporali).

        SALA VII, 4. Madonna with Angels and four Saints.

        5. God, the Father, with Angels and Seraphim.

        6–9, 17. Panels with two Angels in each.

        10. Standard : Christ in Glory, with St. Bernardino, and adoring Perugians below, 1465.

        11, 13, 16, 17. Angels with Baskets of Flowers.

        S. FIORENZO. Standard : Madonna and Saints, 1476.

        S. PIETRO. L. AISLE, END. Pietà, 1469.

ANDREA DEL BRESCIANINO.

Sienese. Active from 1507– after 1525. Probably pupil of Pacchia ; influenced by Beccafumi, Fra Bartolommeo, and Raphael.

Altenburg. Fragment of an Annunciation.
Berlin. 230. Madonna with St. Anne.
Florence. UFFIZI, 1205.bis Madonna and Angels.
        SANTA CROCE, REFECTORY, 4. Assumption of Virgin.
Glasgow. 15A. Adoration of Magi.
Munich. 1075. Madonna.
Siena. SALA X, 8. Predella.
        9. Madonna and Saints.

Siena (*Con.*). PALAZZO PALMIERI-NUTI. Madonna (a version of the Bridgewater Madonna ascribed to Raphael).

 Charity.

 Lucretia.

 Faith.

 PALAZZO SARACINI. Portable votive Shrine.

 Madonna with St. Jerome and Baptist.

 Two tondi : Madonna in each.

 BAPTISTRY, HIGH ALTAR. Baptism (in part), 1524.

 ORATORIO DI S. BERNARDINO, ENTRANCE CHAPEL (GROUND FLOOR). Madonna with SS. John and Bartholomew. E.

Turin. 112. Holy Family.

 ACADEMY ALBERTINA. Holy Family.

COTIGNOLA, *see* ZAGANELLI.

DOMENCIO DI BARTOLO.

Sienese. Circa 1400–1449 ? Pupil of Taddeo di Bartolo.

Asciano. S. AGOSTINO, 2ND ALTAR R. Polyptych, 1437. HIGH ALTAR. Madonna (from same Polyptych).

Perugia. SALA V, 26. Polyptych. 1438.

Siena. SALA III, 19. Madonna, 1433.

 SPEDALE, PELLEGRINAIO. Five Frescoes representing the history and purpose of the Hospital, 1440–1443.

 INFERMERIA DI S. PIETRO. Madonna of Mercy (Fresco).

 INFERMERIA DI S. PIO. Monochromo Fresco : Prayer of Beato Sorore.

Siena *(Con.)*.   Duomo, Pavement (from design).   Emperor
           Sigismond enthroned, 1434.

DUCCIO DI BUONINSEGNA.

Sienese.   Active 1282–1339.   Owes his style to influence of
      the best Byzantine masters of the time : in all probabil-
      ity studied at Constantinople.

Berlin.   1062.^A Triptych.
London.   566. Triptych.
           1139. Annunciation.
           1140. Christ healing the Blind.
           1330. Transfiguration.
           Mr. R. Benson.   Four *Predelle :* Raising of
               Lazarus ; Miraculous Draught ; Christ and
               the Samaritan ; Temptation.

           Lord Crawford.   Crucifixion.
Perugia.   Sala I, 29. Madonna (in part).
Siena.   Sala I, 20. Small Madonna enthroned. E.
               22, 23. Saints (ruined).
               28. Madonna with four Saints.
               35. Triptych.
               47. Polyptych.
           Opera del Duomo.   Reredos, formerly in
               Duomo, 1308–1311.
           Abbazia di S. Eugenio, Sacristy.   Madonna.
           Confraternità della Madonna sotto le
               volte dell' Ospedale.   Crucifixion : En-
               tombment ; Flagellation (originally a Trip-
               tych, now scattered).

EUSEBIO DI SAN GIORGIO.

Umbrian. Active 1492–1527. Pupil of Perugino and Pintoricchio ; influenced by the young Raphael.

Assisi.   S. DAMIANO, Frescoes : Annunciation, **1507.**
St. Francis receiving Stigmata, 1507.
Berlin.   147. Madonna and infant John.
Città di Castello.   16. Creation of Eve.(?)
32. Crucifixion.(?)
Diruta.   S. FRANCESCO, Fresco : Madonna and Saints.
Matelica.   S. FRANCESCO, 4TH CHAPEL R. Madonna and
Saints, 1512.
Perugia.   SALA XI, 15. Madonna and four Saints.
18. Madonna and Saints, 1508.
20. Madonna reading.
23. Adoration of Magi, 1505.
SALA XIII, 16. Madonna and Saints.
SALA XIV. 2. Madonna.
3. The Angel Gabriel.
S. PIETRO, L. AISLE. Adoration of Magi.(?)
Rome.   ACCADEMIA DI S. LUCA. Madonna.

FABRIANO *see* GENTILE.

FIORENZO DI LORENZO.

Umbrian. 1440–1521. Pupil possibly of Benozzo Gozzoli,
but formed under the influence of Niccolò da Foligno
and Ant. Pollaiuolo.

Assisi.   MUNICIPIO. 17. Fresco : Madonna.
S. M. DEGLI ANGELI. Panel on outside wall of
Portiuncula : Annunciation. E.
Berlin   129. Madonna, 1481.

Diruta.   S. ANTONIO.   Madonna of Mercy (Fresco).   E.
Florence.   PITTI, 341.   Adoration of Magi.   L.
Frankfort a/M.   15. Madonna with SS. Sebastian and Chris-
           topher.   E.
Montone.   S. FRANCESCO.   Madonna of Mercy (in small
           part), 1482.
New Haven, U. S. A. JARVES COLLECTION, 60. St. Jerome.
Perugia.   SALA III, 12. Madonna of Mercy.
           SALA VIII, 1. Fresco: Madonna with SS.
           Nicholas and Catherine.
              2. Nativity.   E.
              3. Predella: St. Francis and six other Saints.
              4. Adoration of Magi.   L.
              7. Ornamental Decoration.
              32–43. Polyptych.
              44. Pietà.
           SALA IX, 1–6. Miracles of St. Bernardino, 1473.
              10. Madonna and Saints, with predella.   E.
              11. St. Sebastian.   E.
              12–14. Saints.
              15. Niche with St. Paul R, St. Peter L, and
                 Madonna with Angels above, 1487.
              16. Madonna and Cherubs in a Garland.   E.
              17. Ornamental Name of Jesus.
           SALA XIV, Frescoes :
              12. Madonna of Mercy.
              13. St. Francis.
              14. Nativity.
              44. Madonna and Angels (ruined).
           LENT BY SIGNORA BERTUCCINI : St. Jerome in
              the Desert.
           MUNICIPIO, COUNCIL HALL. Fresco in lunette
              form : Madonna and Angels.
           DUOMO. R. TRANSEPT. Pietà, 1486.
Vienna.   ACADEMY, 1095. Miniature : Madonna and
           Saints in Glory with Worshippers below.

FRANCESCO DI GIORGIO.

Sienese. 1439–1502. Architect, sculptor, and painter. Pupil of Vecchietta.

London.   Mr. C. Butler. Nativity.

            Madonna with SS. Antony Abbot, Jerome, and Angels.

Paris.   1640. Cassone : Rape of Europa.

Richmond.   Sir F. Cook. Small Nativity.

            Profile of Lady wearing Henin.

Siena.   Sala VI, 15. Susanna and the Elders.

            16. Joseph sold by his Brethren.

            17. Joseph and the Wife of Potiphar.

            20. Madonna and Angel.

            21. Annunciation.

            23. Madonna with SS. Peter and Paul.

            24. Madonna with two Saints.

            Sala X, 41. Nativity, 1475.

            44. Coronation, 1471.

            Archivio. Book Covers : Pius II making his Nephew a Cardinal, 1460.

            Madonna appearing over Siena, 1466.

            Abbazia di S. Eugenio, Chapel R. of Altar. Madonna with two Angels.

            S. Domenico, 6th Altar R. Nativity.

BERNARDINO FUNGAI.

Sienese. 1460–1516. Pupil of Giovanni di Paolo ; influenced by Francesco di Giorgio and the Umbrians.

Buda-Pesth. 40. St. John and the Infant Christ.

Chiusi. Duomo, L. Transept. Nativity.

Liverpool. 34. Madonna.

London. 1331. Madonna and Cherubim. Madonna and two Saints (from South Kensington Museum).

Siena.   SALA IX, 1. Madonna nursing Child.

21. Madonna with two Saints.

23. Madonna with two Saints.

24. Madonna.

33. Madonna nursing Child.

SALA X, 30. Altar-Piece, 1512.

45. Assumption of Virgin.

ARCHIVIO. Book Covers : Madonna drawing Ship to Harbour, 1486. Entrance of Emperor Frederick into Siena.

PALAZZO PALMIERI–NUTI. Madonna with St. Jerome and the Baptist.

S. BARTOLOMMEO (CONTRADA DELL' ISTRICE), SACRISTY. Standard : Madonna and two Saints.

CONFRATERNITÀ DELLA MADONNA SOTTO LE VOLTE DELL' OSPEDALE. Madonna with the two St. Catherines, St. Roch, and Antony Abbot.

HOUSE OF ST. CATHERINE, CHAPEL. Triptych : St. Catherine receiving Stigmata, and two Saints.

S. DOMENICO, 6TH ALTAR R. Predella in five scenes.

FONTEGIUSTA, 2ND ALTAR R. Assumption of Virgin.

S. GIROLAMO, NICHE IN CORRIDOR. Assumption of Virgin.

ISTITUTO DEI SORDIMUTI, OLD REFECTORY. Fresco ; Last Supper. L.

SERVI, 2ND CHAPEL L. The Magdalen ; St. Joseph.

CHOIR. Coronation, 1500.

GIROLAMO GENGA.

1476–1551. Pupil of Signorelli ; influenced by Timoteo Viti, Raphael, and Sodoma.

Bergamo. LOCHIS, 238. A Baptism.
Berlin. I, 317. Dispute about Original Sin.
Dresden. 36. Pilaster painted with figures of Saints.
Florence. PITTI, 382. Portrait of Man.
            UFFIZI, 1205. Martyrdom of St. Sebastian.
London. 910. Triumph of Chastity (Fresco).
            SIR H. HOWARTH. Madonna and Infant John.
            MR. MOND. Coriolanus (Fresco).
Milan. BRERA, 202. Madonna and Saints.
Oldenburg. 37. Madonna and Infant John.
Rome. S. CATERINA DA SIENA, VIA GIULIA. Resurrection.
Siena. SALA VIII, 8. Escape of Prisoners.
            9. Escape of Æneas from Troy.
            SALA X, 35. Madonna with SS. John and Antony of Padua.
            SALA XI, 69. Madonna.
            OPERA DEL DUOMO, SALA DELLA SCULTURA. Transfiguration. 1510.
Vienna. COUNT LANCKORONSKI. Battle Scene.

GENTILE DA FABRIANO.

Umbrian. 1360 (?)–1428. Pupil of Alegretto Nuzi.

Berlin. 1130. Madonna, two Saints, and Donor.
Florence. ACADEMY, 165. Adoration of Magi, 1423.
            UFFIZI, 1310. Magdalen, Baptist, and SS. Nicholas of Bari and George, 1425.
Milan. BRERA, 159. Madonna in Glory. **E.**
            190. The Magdalen. **E.**

10

Milan (*Con.*). 194. St. Francis. E.

274. St. Jerome. E.

279. St. Dominic. E.

POLDI-PEZZOLI. Madonna.

New Haven, U. S. A.   JARVES COLLECTION. Madonna.

Orvieto.   DUOMO, L. WALL, Fresco. Madonna, 1425.

Paris.   1278. Presentation in Temple (from altar-piece in Florence Academy), 1423.

Perugia.   SALA V, 39. Madonna.

Pisa.   26. Madonna in Rose Garden.

Rome.   VATICAN, MUSEO CRISTIANO. Head of Charlemagne (fragment of fresco, doubtless from Lateran, 1427).

GIULIO ROMANO.*

1492 (?)–1546. Pupil of Raphael ; influenced by Michelangelo. (Note E stands for pictures done more or less under Raphael's guidance. See also under Raphael.)

Alnwick.   DUKE OF NORTHUMBERLAND. Copy of Raphael's "Madonna with the Pink."

Buda-Pesth.   171. Diana and Endymion.

Dresden.   103. "Madonna della Catina." L.

104. Pan and Olympus.

Genoa.   S. STEFANO. Stoning of Stephen, 1523.

London.   744. "Garvagh Madonna." E.

Madrid.   366. "Lo Spasimo" (in some part by Penni), 1517.

369. "La Perla."

Mantua.   PALAZZO GONZAGA. Decorative Frescoes (executed chiefly by assistants), 1537–1538.

PALAZZO DEL TÈ. Frescoes : Story of Cupid and Psyche.

Fall of Giants and other Frescoes (in great part), 1532–1534.

* More important works only.

Munich.   1087. Bust of an Ecclesiastic.
Naples.   SALA GRANDE, 5. "Madonna della Gatta."
                22. "Madonna col Divin' Amore."
Parma.   371. Madonna in Glory and Saints.
Paris.   1418. Nativity, 1531.
                1420. Triumph of Venus and Vespasian. L.
                1421. Venus and Vulcan.
                1422. Portrait of Man.
                1438. Circumcision. L.
                1497. "Vierge au Voile." E.
                1498. "Sainte Famille de François I," 1518.
                1504. St. Michael crushing Satan, 1518.
                1507. Portrait of Giovanna d' Aragona, 1518.
                1508. Portraits of two Men.
Rome.   BARBERINI, 86. "La Fornarina."
                BORGHESE, 374. Madonna and Infant John.
                CAPITOL, 71. Judith.
                VATICAN. Gallery. Lower part of Raphael's
                Transfiguration. Upper part of a Corona-
                tion (lower by Penni). Finished. 1525.
                SALA DEL CONSTANTINO. Frescoes : Battle of
                Ponte Molle ; Constantine addressing his
                Troops, 1524.
                MISS H. HERTZ. Madonna. E.
                S. M. DELL' ANIMA. Altar-piece : Madonna and
                Saints.
                S. PRASSEDE, Socristy. Flagellation.
Vienna.   31. St. Margaret.

LIPPO MEMMI.

?–1357 (?).   Pupil and assistant of Simone Martini.

Aix-en-Provence.   Small Annunciation and Nativity.
Altenburg. Small Madonna.

Asciano.   S. Francesco, Chapel L. of Choir. Madonna
and Donor.   L.

Berlin.   1067, 1072, 1081^A.   Madonnas.
Herr Kaufmann.   Small Crucifixion.
Large Madonna.

Buda-Pesth.   9. Small Madonna.

Cologne.   741–750.   Busts of Apostles.

Florence.   Signor Bardini.   Small Madonna, with Frieze
of Saints below.

Munich.   986.   Triptych.

Orvieto.   Duomo, Chapel of L. Transept.   Madonna
of Mercy.   L.
Opera del Duomo, 3.   Madonna with Saints
and Angels.

Rome.   Vatican, Museo Cristiano, Case H, VI.
Small Crucifixion, with six Saints below.

San Gimignano.   Municipio.   Fresco : Madonna and many
Saints, 1317.   (Two figures to R. com-
pletely repainted by Benozzo Gozzoli, 1467).

Siena.   S. M. dei Servi, Over Sacristy Door.
Madonna.

AMBROGIO LORENZETTI.

Active 1323–1348.   Pupil of his elder brother Pietro ; influenced by works of Giovanni Pisano and Giotto.

Florence.   Academy, 132.   Two stories from Legend of St.
Nicholas of Bari, 1332.
134. Presentation, 1342.

London.   1147. Heads of Nuns (Fresco), 1331.

Rome.   Vatican, Museo Cristiano, Case C, VI–XIII.
Predelle pictures.

Siena.   Sala II, 2, Polyptych : Madonna, Saints, and
Entombment.

AMBROGIO LORENZETTI 149

Siena *(Con.)*. 9. Madonna and Saints, 1326.

> 33. Annunciation, 1344.
> 34. St. Antony Abbot.
> 36. St. Maximin.

> ARCHIVIO. Book cover: Symbolical figure of Commune, 1344. (?)

> OPERA DEL DUOMO, 69–73. Four Saints.

> PALAZZO PUBBLICO, SALA DELLA PACE. Frescoes: Good and Bad Government, 1338–1440.

> LOGGIA. Fresco: Madonna.

> ABBAZIA DI S. EUGENIO, CHAPEL L. OF CHOIR. Madonna.

> S. FRANCESCO. CHAPEL OPENING FROM R. TRANSEPT. Madonna. 3RD CHAPEL L. OF CHOIR. Frescoes: St. Francis before the Pope (ruined); Martyrdom of Saints (ruined). All 1331.

> SERVI, CHAPEL L. OF CHOIR. Frescoes: Salome, and Ascension of John the Evangelist (ruined) (?).

PIETRO LORENZETTI.

Active 1305–1348. Pupil of Simone Martini; influenced by Giovanni Pisano.

Arezzo. PIEVE. Polypytch : Madonna and Saints, 1320.

Assisi. S. FRANCESCO, LOWER CHURCH. L. TRANSEPT. All the frescoes on the walls and vaulting, representing the Madonna with SS. Francis and Louis; scenes from the Passion; and various single figures of Saints.

> APSE OF L. TRANSEPT. Triptych: Madonna with St. Francis and the Baptist.

Berlin.   1077. St. Humilitas heals a sick Nun, 1316.
            1077^A. Death of St. Humilitas, 1316.
Buda-Pesth.   22. Madonna enthroned.
Cortona.   DUOMO, 3RD ALTAR R.   Madonna and Angels,
            S. MARCO.   Painted Crucifix.
Florence.   ACADEMY, 133.   Story of St. Humilitas, 1316.
            UFFIZI, 15.   Madonna, 1315.
            16. Thebaid.
Milan.   POLDI-PEZZOLI.   113. Madonna and Angels.
Münster in W. 2. Madonna and Saints.
Rome.   S. LUCIA, PILLAR R. OF CHOIR.   Small Ma-
            donna.
            VATICAN, MUSEO CRISTIANO, CASE E, X. Small
            Madonna with female Saints.
S. Ansano in Dofana (Province of Siena).   CHURCH.
            Altar-piece : Madonna with St. Nicholas of
            Bari, Antony Abbot, and Angels, 1328.
Siena.   SALA II, 5.   Madonna in Glory.
            21.   Madonna and Angels.
            28, 29.   Parts of a *Predella*.
            37.   Religious Allegory (?),
            OPERA DEL DUOMO.   63.   Birth of Virgin. 1342.
            S. FRANCESCO, 1ST CHAPEL L. OF CHOIR.
            Fresco : Crucifixion.
            CHAPEL OPENING FROM R. TRANSEPT.   Fresco
            in form of Polyptych (ruined).
            S. PIETRO OVILE, LEFT WALL.   Madonna.
            SERVI, CHAPEL R.   Fresco : Massacre of the
            Innocents.

UNKNOWN FOLLOWER OF THE LOREN-ZETTI.

Pisa.   CAMPO SANTO.   Frescoes : Triumph of Death,
            Last Judgment.

Pisa (*Con.*). Thebaïd.

Ascension.

Resurrection.

Incredulity of Thomas.

Crucifixion.

LORENZO DI SAN SEVERINO (the Younger).

Umbrian. —1503. Pupil of Niccolò d'Alùnno ; influenced by Crivelli.

Altenburg. 2. Magadalen and Baptist.

London. 249. Marriage of St. Catherine.

Pausola. COLLEGIATA, Madonna and Saints (Polyptych), 1481.

Rome. CORSINI, 709. Madonna and two Saints.

VATICAN, Museo CRISTIANO, Case S, VIII. Adoration of Magi.

PRINCE COLONNA. Large Madonna.

Sarnano. COLLEGIATA. Madonna and Saints (Polyptych), 1483.

LORENZO DI VITERBO.

Circa 1446–1470. Developed under the influence of Benozzo Gozzoli.

Viterbo. S. MARIA DELLA VERITÀ, CAPPELLA MAZZA- TOSTA. Presentation of Virgin ; Sposalizio ; Nativity, and other Frescoes. Finished 1469.

GIANNICOLO MANNI.*

Umbrian. Active 1493–1544. Pupil of Perugino and Pinto- ricchio, influenced by Raphael and later by Sodoma.

* Only better works are mentioned here.

Città della Pieve.   Duomo, Choir.   Madonna and Saints.
      Altar L.   Baptism.

Cologne.   730^K.   Madonna and Saints. (?)

Florence.   Signor Bardini.   Four nude Men (fragment).
      Palazzo Torrigiani.   Three Cassone pictures :
      Mythological scenes. E. (?)

Frankfort a/M. 16.   Madonna and Infant John (Copy of a
      Perugino).

London.   1104.   Annunciation.

Paris.   1369.   Baptism.
      1370.   Assumption of Virgin.
      1371.   Adoration of Magi.
      1372.   Holy Family and Saints.

Perugia.   Sala XII, 27.   SS. Bernardino and Sebastian.
      28.   Martyrdom of four Saints.
      29.   SS. Costanzo and Ercolano.
      30.   Polyptych.   E.
      Sala XIII, 6.   Holy Family and Saints.
      40.   Resurrection.   L.
      Sala XV, 2.   SS. Roch and Sebastian.
      8.   Christ in Garden.
      Cambio, Chapel.   Altar-piece : Baptism and
      Annunciation.   Frescoes on Ceiling and
      Wall, 1515–1518.
      S. Pietro, Choir.   Lunette.

BERNARDINO DI MARIOTTO.

Umbrian.   Active 1497–1525. Pupil of Fiorenzo di Lorenzo,
  influenced by Signorelli but more by Lorenzo di S.
  Severino, the Younger, and by Crivelli.

Altenburg.   Madonna crowned by two Angels, adoring Child,
     with SS. Francis and Jerome.

La Bastia (near Fabriano).   Church.   Madonna, 1498.

Bergamo. MORELLI, 55. Deposition.

Berlin. (In Magazine) Madonna and two Angels (tondo).

Chalons s/M. 497. Madonna.

Gualdo-Tadino. DUOMO, SACRISTY. Madonna in Glory.

London. DR. J. P. RICHTER. St. Lawrence.
St. Andrew.

Paris. M. FOULKE. Madonna saving a Child from Demon. E.

Perugia. SALA VII, 1. Marriage of St. Catherine.
2. Madonna and Saints.
3. Coronation of Virgin.
20. Madonna with SS. Andrew and Julian.
21. Marriage of St. Catherine.

Richmond. SIR. F. COOK. Visitation, Presentation.

Rome. VATICAN, MUSEO CRISTIANO, CASE T, I–III.
Triptych : Madonna and Saints, 1497.
DON MARCELLO MASSARENTI. Madonna.
PRINCE COLONNA. Christ among the Doctors.
Nativity.

San Severino. PINACOTECA. 6. Annunciation, 1514.
7. Entombment.
8. Entombment.
DUOMO, SACRISTY. Madonna saving a Child from Demon, 1509.
S. DOMENICO. Madonna and five Saints, 1512.

MARTINI *see* SIMONE.

MATTEO DI GIOVANNI.

Sienese. About 1435–1495. Pupil of Domenico di Bartolo ; strongly influenced by Sano di Pietro.

Aix-en-Provence. 138. Massacre of the Innocents. (?)

Asciano. COLLEGIATA, L. TRANSEPT. St. Michael and
a Bishop (to R. and L. of an Assumption by
Giovanni di Paolo).

Ashridge. LORD BROWNLOW. Two episodes from Life of
St. Jerome.

Bergamo. MORELLI, 54. Madonna.

Brighton. MR. HENRY WILLETT. Madonna with St.
Michael and the Baptist.

Buonconvento. SS. PIETRO E PAOLO, HIGH ALTAR. Madonna.

London. 247. Ecce Homo.
1155. Assumption of Virgin.
1461. St. Sebastian.
MR. C. BUTLER. Three cassone pictures :
Judgment of Paris ; Queen Camilla ; Solomon and Queen of Sheba. Madonna and
two Angels.
MR. Mond. Profile bust of Lady.

Meiningen. Madonna and Saints.

Munich. 6. Portrait of Braccio Fortebracci.

Naples. SALA TOSCANA, 31. Massacre of the Innocents.

Paris. M. CHABRIÈRES ARLÈS. Cassone : Solomon and
the Queen of Sheba.

Pienza. DUOMO, R. TRANSEPT. Madonna and four
Saints. E.
L. TRANSEPT. Madonna and four Saints.

Rome. VATICAN, MUSEO CRISTIANO, CASE N, XIV.
St. Barbara.
CASE Q, IV. Story of St. James.

Siena. SALA VI, 5, 6. Madonnas, Saints, and Angels.
7. Madonna enthroned with four Angels.
1470.
9. Madonna.
12. Madonna and Saints. (?)
SALA X, 17. Lunette : Nativity.
SALA, 36. Madonna enthroned with four
Saints, and four Angels.

Siena) *Con.*). OPERA DEL DUOMO, 64. Madonna, Saints, and
Angels.

Long *Predella* with five Scenes.

BELCARO. Madonna and two Saints.

PALAZZO PALMIERI-NUTI. Madonna and two
Angels.

S. DOMENICO, 6TH ALTAR R. Lunette : Pietà.

2ND CHAPEL L. OF CHOIR. St. Barbara
enthroned with Saints.

Lunette ; Adoration, 1479.

3RD CHAPEL L. OF CHOIR. Triptych :
Madonna, Baptist, and St. Jerome.

DUOMO, PAVEMENT (from design). Massacre of
Innocents, 1481. Samian Sibyl, 1483.

MADONNA DELLE NEVE. Madonna and Saints,
and three predelle, 1477.

S. PIETRO OVILE, L. WALL. St. Bernardino and
the Baptist (to R. and L. of a Madonna by
Pietro Lorenzetti).

S. SEBASTIANO IN VALLE PIATTA, SACRISTY.
Madonna with the Baptist, St. Jerome, and
two Angels.

SERVI, 4TH ALTAR R. Massacre of Innocents.
147 (or 9) I. Lunette : Madonna, Saints, and
Donors.

MELOZZO DA FORLÌ.

1438–1494. Pupil of Piero dei Franceschi.

Forlì. PINACOTECA. Fresco : " Pesta-Pepe."

Loreto. SANTA CASA, R. SACRISTY. Frescoes : CUPOLA,
Prophets and Angels ; WALL, Entry into
Jerusalem. (Execution of the whole almost
entirely by Palmezzano.)

Rome. COLONNA, 135. Profile Bust of Boy in Red.

Rome (*Con.*). VATICAN.   Fresco : Sixtus IV. and his Court.
QUIRINAL, STAIRCASE.   Christ Ascending (frag-
ment of frescoes once in the cupola of Santi
Apostoli).
ST. PETER'S, INNER SACRISTY.   Music-making
Angels, Apostles, and Cherubs (fragments
of frescoes once in the cupola of Santa
Apostoli).

MEMMI *see* LIPPO.

NEROCCIO DI LANDI.

Sienese.   1447–1500.   Sculptor and Painter.   Pupil of Vec-
chietta.
Bergamo.   MORELLI, 47.   Madonna.
Berlin.   63ᴬ.   Madonna and Saints.
Florence.   UFFIZI, 1304.   Predella : Episodes from Life of
St. Benedict.
Frankfort a/M.   4.   Madonna and two Saints.
5ᴀ.   Madonna with SS. Catherine and Sebastian.
London.   MR. C. BUTLER.   Madonna.
Meiningen. Holy Family.
New Haven, U. S. A. JARVES COLLECTION, 65.   An-
nunciation.
Paris.   M. G. DREYFUS.   Claudia.
M. MARTIN LE ROY.   Tobias and the Angel.
Siena.   SALA VI, 8.   Madonna with six Saints, 1492.
11.   Madonna with SS. Bernardino and Jerome.
13.   Madonna with SS. Catherine and Bernardino.
14.   Madonna with SS. Catherine and Jerome.
19.   Triptych, 1476.
22.   Madonna with two Saints.
SALA VII, 2.   Cassone : Triumph of David.
8.   Fragment of an Annunciation.

Siena *(Con.)*. ARCHIVIO. Book cover : Madonna protecting
Siena, 1480.

> PALAZZO SARACINI. Madonna with St. Cath-
> erine and the Magdalen. Madonna with
> Baptist and the Magdalen.

> CONFRATERNITA DELLA SS. TRINITÀ, SACRISTY
> UPSTAIRS. Madonna with St. Michael and
> the Baptist.

> DUOMO, PAVEMENT (from design). Hellespon-
> tine Sibyl, 1483.

NICCOLÒ DA FOLIGNO (ALUNNO.)

About 1430–1502. Pupil of Benozzo Gozzoli ; at the end of
his career slightly influenced by Crivelli.

Assisi. DUOMO. Triptych.

La Bastia (near Assisi). Triptych with predella, 1499.

Bayeux. 27.ᴬ. Pietà.

Bergamo. MORELLI, 6. Head of Saint.

Bologna. Standard : on one side, Annunciation ; on the
other, Madonna and Saints, 1482.

Buda-Pesth. 37. St. Bernardino, 1497.

Diruta. SIGNORA G. C. MORGANTI. Standard painted
on both sides.

Foligno. S. BARTOLOMMEO. Martyrdom of St. Bartholomew (in part ; left unfinished at death).

> S. MARIA IN CAMPIS. Fresco : Crucifixion,
> 1456.

> S. MARIA INFRA PORTIS. Frescoes : Christ
> bearing Cross ; St. Roch and Angels.

> S. NICCOLÒ. Polyptych, 1492.
> Coronation and Saints.

Gualdo-Tadino. PINACOTECA. Polyptych, 1471.

> DUOMO, SACRISTY. Polyptych.

Karlsruhe. 403. Panel in two compartments, 1468.

ᶠ

London.   1107. Polyptych with scenes from the Passion,
                    1487.
Milan.   BRERA, 160. St. Louis of Toulouse.
                    161. Christ on Cross adored by Angels.
                    180. Madonna and Angels, 1465.
                    165. Four Saints.
                    183. St. Bernardino, 1465.
                    200. St. Francis, 1465.
                    276. Female Saint.
                    278. St. Peter Martyr.
Montefalco. PINACOTECA. Scene from Crucifixion.
Nocera.   DUOMO, SACRISTY. Polyptych, 1483.
Paris.   1120. Scenes from the Passion, 1492.
Perugia.   ENTRANCE HALL. Madonna and Angels, 1458.
               SALA VII. 14. Annunciation, 1466.
Rome.   VILLA ALBANI. Polyptych, 1475.
               COLONNA, 39. Madonna saving a Child from
                    Demon.
               VATICAN, Polyptych, 1466.
               Polyptych.
San Severino. CHIESA DEL CASTELLO. Polyptych, 1468.
               S. LORENZO. 3ᵈ Altar, R. Nativity and Donor.
Terni.   MUNICIPIO. Crucifixion, 1497.

GIROLAMO DEL PACCHIA.

Sienese. 1477–after 1535. Pupil of Fungai ; influenced by
     Fra Bartolommeo, Sodoma, Andrea del Sarto, Raphael,
     and Genga.

Berlin.   105. Sposalizio.
               HERR BECKERATH. Santa Conversazione.
               HERR WESENDONCK, 4½. Madonna.
Brighton. MR. HENRY WILLETT. Madonna.
Buda-Pesth. 53. Madonna with St. Francis.
London.   246. Madonna.
Munich.   1058. Madonna with two Angels.

Munich (*Con.*). 1059. St. Bernardino and Angels.

Naples. Scuola Romana, 26. Madonna and Infant John.

Paris. 1642. Crucifixion. L. (?)

Scotland. New Battle, Marquis of Lothian. Madonna in Landscape, reading.

Siena. Sala VIII, 12. Madonna with SS. Catherine and Jerome.

> 30. Madonna with Infant John.

> Sala X, 7. Annunciation and Visitation, 1518.

> Palazzo Palmieri-Nuti. Dead Christ.

> Palazzo Saracini. Madonna with St. Nicholas of Bari and another Bishop.

> Baptistery, Lunette under R. Arch. Fresco ; Marriage of Cana. E.

> S. Cristofero. Madonna and Saints. L.

> S. Donato, 2d Altar, L. Madonna.

> S. Girolamo, 2d Altar, L. Frescoes ; two Saints to R. and L. of Altar ; Above, St. Jerome in his Study.

> Oratorio della Contrada dell' Oca. Frescoes : St. Catherine healing Rector of Hospital ; St. Catherine at the Funeral of St. Agnes of Montepulciano ; St. Catherine rescuing Monks from Robbers. (Over Altar) St. Catherine receiving the Stigmata (?)

> Oratory of St. Bernardino. Frescoes : Birth of Virgin ; Annunciation ; St. Bernardino ; St. Antony of Padua.

> S. Spirito. 3d Altar, L. Coronation and Saints.

Turin. 115. Madonna and Angels.

Vienna. 37. Annunciation (?).

GIACOMO PACCHIAROTTO.

Sienese. 1474–1540. Pupil of Fungai ; influenced by Matteo di Giovanni and Francesco di Giorgio.

Buonconvento. SS Pietro e Paolo, Sacristy, Madonna and
four Saints. E.
Florence. Academy, 81. Visitation.
London. Mr. C. Butler. Four small panels : Nativity ;
Baptism ; Resurrection ; Pentecost,
Mr. Muir Mackenzie. Moses, David, and
other prophets.
Rome. Don Marcello Massarenti. Crucifixion.
Scotland. Rossie Priory, Lord Kinnaird. Nativity.
Siena. Sala IX, 5. Five Saints,
Sala X. 14. Madonna and Saints ; in lunette
Christ with SS. Jerome and Francis.
23. Predella. E.
24. Altar-piece : Ascension. E.
31. Visitation. E.
Palazzo Palmieri-Nuti, Holy Family. Ma-
donna with St. Jerome and a female Saint.
Carmine, 4th Altar R. Ascension.

MARCO PALMEZZANO.*

About 1456–after 1543. Pupil of Melozzo da Forlì ; influenced by Rondinelli.

Berlin. Annunciation.
131. Nativity
1087. Madonna and Saints.
1129. Christ bearing Cross, 1503.
1129ᴬ. Resurrected Christ, 1515.
Bologna. Madonna and Child.
Brescia. Gal. Martinengo, Sala C. I. Christ bearing
Cross.
Bulciago. Church. Altar-piece, 1481.
Casate Nuovo. Church. Altar-piece.
Dijon. 32. Madonna and Saints.
Faenza. Altar-piece and Lunette.

* Better works only.

Faenza (*Con.*). Christ bearing Cross.
Tobias and the Angel.
St. Jerome,
St. Augustin.

Florence. UFFIZI, 1095. Crucifixion.

Forli. 125. St. Helena, 1516.
120. Annunciation. E.
117. Crucifixion (fresco).
119. St. Antony Abbot between St. Sebastian and the Baptist. E.
121. God the Father. E.
113. Annunciation.
143. Madonna.
124. Madonna and Saints. E.
116. Christ bearing Cross, 1535.
122. Communion of Apostles, 1501.
114. Portrait of Himself, 1536.
110. "Cesare Borgia."
111. Circumcision.
112. Flight into Egypt.

S. BIAGIO e GIROLAMO, 1ST CHAPEL R. Frescoes: CUPOLA, Prophets and putti, E. LUNETTE, Legendary Subject, E. ; WALL, Martyrdom of St. James.

4TH CHAPEL R. Triptych ; Frescoes in Cupola.

S. MERCURIALE, 3D ALTAR, R. Madonna in Glory, with two Saints and a Donor worshipping a Crucifix.

5TH ALTAR, R. Madonna enthroned between Magdalen and the Baptist.

4TH CHAPEL, L. Altar-piece ; Conception ; Lunette : Dead Christ ; predelle.

Hamburg. CONSUL WEBER, 25. Madonna and two Saints.

Karlsruhe. 405. St. Sebastian.

Liverpool. 29. Madonna and six Saints.

11

London. 596. Pietà, 1501.

Matelica. S. Francesco. Polyptych: Madonna and Saints, 1501.

Meiningen. Madonna, Infant John, and Antony Abbot.

Milan. Brera, 178. Coronation.

185. Madonna and Saints, 1493.

197. Nativity, 1492.

Munich. 1026. Madonna and Saints, 1513.

Padua. Sala Romanino, 673. Holy Family with Infant John, 1536.

Madonna with Infant John.

Paris. 1400. Dead Christ, 1510.

Ravenna. 305. Circumcision.

316. Nativity.

Rome. Lateran, 67. Annunciation.

76. Madonna with Saints and Angels, 1510.

80. Madonna with Saints and Angels, 1537.

Venice. Correr, Sala VI, 24. Christ bearing Cross.

Vicenza. Sala IV, 20. Dead Christ.

Vienna. Academy, 1098. Bust of Young Man.

1125. Madonna with St. Jerome and a Donor.

PIETRO PERUGINO.

Umbrian. 1446–1524. Pupil of Fiorenzo di Lorenzo; influenced by Signorelli and slightly by Verrocchio.

Altenburg. St. Helen. L.

St. Antony of Padua. L.

Alnwick. Duke of Northumberland. Two female Saints. L.

Assisi. S. M. degli Angeli. Fresco behind Portiuncula: Scene at foot of Cross.

Bassano. Cabinet, R. 28. Small Deposition.

Bettona. Pieve. St. Antony of Padua and Donor, 1512.

Bologna. Madonna appearing to four Saints.

Borgo San Sepolcro. Duomo. Ascension (in part).

Città della Pieve. Duomo. Madonna appearing to four Saints, 1513.

   S. Maria. Fresco: Deposition, 1517.

   S. M. dei Bianchi. Fresco: Adoration of Magi, 1504.

   S. Pietro. Fresco: St. Antony Abbot enthroned.

Cremona. S. Agostino. Madonna and Saints, 1494.

Fano. S. M. Nuova. 3d Altar, R. Altar-piece: Madonna and Saints; Pietà (in lunette); predelle, 1497.

   2d Altar, L. Annunciation.

Florence. Academy, 53. Agony in Garden.

   56. Pietà. E.

   57. Assumption of Virgin, 1500.

   78. Christ on Cross and Saints.

   98. Deposition (begun by Filippino), 1505.

   241. Portrait of Dom Blasio, 1500.

   242. Portrait of Dom Balthazar, 1500.

   Pitti, 164. Entombment, 1495.

   219. Madonna adoring Child.

   Uffizi, 287. Portrait of Francesco dell' Opere, 1494.

   1120. Portrait of a Lady.

   1122. Madonna and Saints, 1493.

   1217. Portrait of Alessandro Braccesi.

   Via Faenza. Fresco: "Cena di Foligno" (about 1490; in part).

   SS. Annunziata, 4th Altar, L. Assumption, 1506.

   La Calza, High Altar. Crucifixion and Saints. E.

   S. M. Maddalena dei Pazzi. Fresco: Crucifixion, 1493–1496.

Florence (*Con.*). S. Spirito, W. Window. Ascension (after design).

Foligno.   SS. Annunziata. Fresco : Baptism. **L.**

Frankfort a/M.   16. Madonna and Infant John.

London.   181. Madonna and Infant John.

288. Triptych.

1075. Madonna and Saints. **L.**

1441. Fresco : Nativity, 1522.

Dorchester House. Madonna (?).

Mr. Muir Mackenzie. Head of Madonna.

Lord Wantage. St. Jerome.

St. Sebastian.

Lyons.   45. Ascension, 1496.

46. A Bishop and a Saint. **L.**

Marseilles. 331. Holy Family and Saints. **L.**

Meiningen. Ducal Palace. The Baptist. **L.**

John the Evangelist. **L.**

Montefalco. S. Francesco, Niche L. of Door. Fresco : Nativity.

Munich.   1034. Vision of St. Bernard.

1035. Madonna and two Saints. **L.**

Nancy.   Madonna and Angels, 1515.

Naples.   Sala Grande, 11. Adoration of Magi. Madonna in Landscape (?)

Duomo. Assumption (in small part).

Panicale.   S. Sebastiano. Fresco : Martyrdom of St. Sebastian, 1505.

Paris.   1509. Apollo and Marsyas.

1564. Holy Family (tondo). **E.**

1565. Holy Family.

1566. St. Paul. **L.**

1567. Combat of Love and Chastity, 1505.

St. Sebastian (small). **L.**

St. Sebastian (large). **E.**

St. Gervais. Lunette : God the Father and Cherubs, 1495.

Perugia. SALA X, 1. St. Jerome and the Magdalen.

2. St. Sebastian (in part), 1518.

4. S. Giacomo della Marca.

5. St. Jerome.

6. God and Seraphim.

6bis. Fragment of Predella, 1495.

7. Preaching of Baptist. L.

8, 9, 13, 14, 17, 18, 22, 23. Various Saints. L.

10. Pietà.

11. Baptism. L.

12. Marriage of Cana. L.

15. David. L.

16. Christ in the Temple. L.

19. Daniel. L.

20. Nativity. L.

21. Adoration of Magi. L.

24. Madonna and Saints.

25. Crucifixion. Ordered 1502 ; executed later.

26. Archangel Gabriel.

SALA XI, 2. Transfiguration, 1522.

3. Annunciation, 1522.

4. Nativity, 1522.

5. Baptism, 1522.

6. Madonna and Angels, 1498.

14. Madonna and Angels appearing to Saints.

16. Six Saints.

SALA XIII, 31. Fresco : Nativity. L.

CAMBIO. Frescoes, 1500.

S. PIETRO, SACRISTY. Five Saints (half length), 1495.

L. WALL. Pietà. L.

S. SEVERO. Frescoes : Saints (under Raphael's Trinity), 1521.

Rome. VATICAN, GALLERY. Resurrection. L.

Madonna and four Saints, 1496.

Three Heads, 1495.

Rome (*Con.*). SIXTINE CHAPEL.   Fresco : Christ giving Keys
to Peter, 1482.

STANZA DELL' INCENDIO DEL BORGO.   Ceiling
Frescoes.

VILLA ALBANI. Triptych, 1491.

Rouen.   473. Adoration of Magi, 1495.

474. Baptism, 1495.

492. Resurrection, 1495.

Siena.   S. AGOSTINO.   Crucifixion.   L.

Sinigaglia. S. M. DELLE MISERICORDIE.   CHOIR. Madonna
and Saints (finished by Lo Spagna).

Spello.   COLLEGIATA.   Frescoes R. and L. of Choir.
Pietà ; Madonna with SS. Catherine and
Biagio, 1521.

Toulouse. 36. Two Saints (pendant to Lyons, No. 46).   L.

Trevi.   S. M. DELLE LAGRIME.   Fresco : Epiphany,
1521.

Vienna.   25. St. Jerome.

27. Madonna and four Saints, 1493.

BALDASSARE PERUZZI.

Sienese. 1481-1537. Pupil, probably, of Pacchiarotto, assistant of Pintoricchio ; influenced by Sodoma and Raphael.   More renowned as Architect.

Berlin.   (MAGAZINE) 98. Annunciation.   E. (?)

Chiusi.   DUOMO, SACRISTY.   Madonna and Saints.

Dresden.   99. Adoration of Magi.

London.   BRIDGEWATER HOUSE. Adoration of Magi.

MR. MOND. Portrait of Alberto Pio da Carpi,
1512.

Madrid.   573. Rape of Sabines.   E.

574. Continence of Scipio.   E.

Milan.   MARCHESE FASSATI. Bust of Young Man.

CONTE GIOVIO. Dido and Æneas.

Montpellier. 577. Bust of Young Man.

Munich. 1052. Portrait of " Bindo Altoviti."

Münster in W. 40. Madonna and Infant John. E.

Rome. VILLA ALBANI. Madonna with SS. Lawrence, Sebastian, James, and Donor. E.

BORGHESE, 92. Venus.

CAPITOL. Frescoes: SALA IV, Judith ; Roman Triumph. E.

SALA VII. Hannibal in Italy.

CORSINI, 706. Flight into Egypt.

FARNESINA, Frescoes : SALA DI GALATEA, the entire ceiling, and in a lunette a gigantic Head in monochrome.

ROOM OFF SALA DI PSICHE. Frieze. All about 1511.

SALOON (upper floor). Decorative Frescoes.

VATICAN, STANZA DELL' ELIODORO, Fresco decoration of ceiling. (Decorative work only).

MUSEO CRISTIANO, CASE S, XIII. Marriage of St. Catherine. E.

PRINCE CHIGI. Fresco : The Three Graces.

S. CROCE IN GERUSALEMME, CRYPT, Mosaics (after design), not later than 1508.

S. M. DELLA PACE, 1ST CHAPEL L. Frescoes : Madonna with Saints and Ponzetti as Donor ; (above) Biblical Scenes, 1516.

R. OF HIGH ALTAR. Presentation of Virgin.

S. ONOFRIO, CHOIR, Frescoes : Assumption and other sacred subjects. E.

S. PIETRO IN MONTORIO, OVER 2D AND 3D CHAPELS, R. Frescoes : Coronation, and Virtues.

Siena. SALA IX, 29. Madonna and Infant John. E.

ARCO DELLE DUE PORTE. Fresco : Madonna, Infant John, and Catherine. L.

Siena (*Con.*). BELCARO (near Siena). Frescoes : CEILING, GROUND FLOOR, Judgment.

LOGGIA, Decorations (completely modernized).

CHURCH, APSE. Madonna and Saints. All 1535.

PALAZZO POLLINI, Ceiling Frescoes : Continence of Scipio ; Epiphany ; Stoning of Elders. L.

DUOMO, CHAPEL OF S. GIOVANNI, Frescoes : Youthful Baptist in Desert ; St. John Preaching, 1501.

FONTEGIUSTA, 1ST ALTAR, L. Augustus and the Sibyl. L.

PIERO DEI FRANCESCHI

1416–1492. Pupil of Domenico Veneziano ; influenced by Paolo Uccello.

Arezzo.   DUOMO, L. TRANSEPT. Fresco : The Magdalen.

S. FRANCESCO, CHOIR. Frescos : Story of True Cross.

Berlin.   View through Colonnade of Piazza stretching down to Sea.

Borgo San Sepolcro. MUNICIPIO. Frescoes : Resurrection ; St. Louis.

OSPEDALE, Polyptych. Ordered 1445.

CONTE COLLACCHIONE, Fresco : Hercules.

Città di Castello. PINACOTECA. Salvator Mundi. L.

Florence.   UFFIZI, 1300. Portraits of Federigo di Montefeltro and his wife, Battista Sforza. On back two Allegories, 1465.

London.   665. Baptism.

908. Nativity.

Milan.   BRERA, 187. Madonna, Saints, and Angels, with Duke of Urbino.

Monterchio. CHAPEL OF CEMETERY. Fresco : Madonna
and two Angels.

New York, U. S. A. HISTORICAL SOCIETY, 180. Triumph
of Chivalry. E.

Perugia. SALA V, 21ᴮ , Lunette containing Annunciation.

Rimini. S. FRANCESCO. Fresco : Sigismondo Malatesta
and his Patron Saint, 1451.

Sinigaglia. S. M. DELLE GRAZIE. Madonna and two Angels
(in great part).

Urbino. 18. Architectural Scene.

DUOMO, SACRISTY. Flagellation.

Venice. 47. St. Jerome with kneeling figure of Girolamo
Amadio.

PIERINO *see* VAGA.

BERNARDO PINTORICCHIO.

Umbrian. 1454–1513. Pupil of Fiorenzo di Lorenzo ; influenced by Signorelli.

Assisi. S. MARIA DEGLI ANGELI, CHAPEL OF S. BONA-
VENTURA. God the Father.

Berlin. 132ᴬ. Reliquary : Three Saints.

Buda-Pesth. 62. Madonna and Cherubs. (?)

Dresden. 41. Portrait of a Boy.

Leipzig. 480. St. Michael. (?)

London. 693. St. Catherine of Alexandria.

703. Madonna.

903. Return of Ulysses (fresco). L.

Milan. BORROMEO. SALA CIMBALLO, 36. Christ bearing Cross, 1513.

PRINCE PIO DI SAVOIA, Madonna, 1497.

MARCHESE VISCONTI-VENOSTA, Small painted
Crucifix.

Oxford. TAYLORIAN, 22. Portrait of Young Man. (?)

Paris. 1417. Madonna with St. Gregory and another
Saint.

Perugia.   SALA XI, 10. Polyptych, 1498.
　　　　　　　12. St. Augustin, 1500.

Rome.   BORGHESE, 377. St. Christopher.   E. (?)
　　　　CAPITOL, SALA VI. Fresco :   Madonna and
　　　　　　　Angels.
　　　　CASTLE OF S. ANGELO. Slight fragments of fres-
　　　　　　　coes, 1495.
　　　　VATICAN, GALLERY. Coronation, 1505.
　　　　　　BORGIA APARTMENT. Frescoes : All done un-
　　　　　　　　der his guidance, 1492–1494 ; only the fol-
　　　　　　　　ing, however, bear traces of his own hand.
　　　　　　　FIRST ROOM (beginning East entrance). As-
　　　　　　　　sumption (in great part) ; Annunciation (in
　　　　　　　　great part) ; Nativity (in small part) ; Res-
　　　　　　　　urrection (only the portrait of Alexander
　　　　　　　　VI).
　　　　　　　SECOND ROOM. Stories of SS. Giuliana, Bar-
　　　　　　　　bara, Antony Abbot, and the Hermit Paul
　　　　　　　　(in great part) ; Visitation, St. Catherine
　　　　　　　　disputing with the Doctors (entirely by
　　　　　　　　him) ; Ceiling decorations (in small part).
　　　　　　　THIRD ROOM. Arithmetic, Geometry (both
　　　　　　　　in great part).
　　　　　　SIXTINE CHAPEL. Frescoes : Journey of Moses
　　　　　　　　to Egypt.   Baptism (both 1482)*.
　　　　　　BELVEDERE. GALLERIA DELLE STATUE. Frag-
　　　　　　　ment of decorative frescoes, 1487.
　　　　PRINCE COLONNA, GROUND FLOOR OF PALACE.
　　　　　　　Decorative frescoes in spandrils.
　　　　PALAZZO DEI PENITENZIERI. Fragments of
　　　　　　　decorative frescoes, 1490.
　　　　ARACŒLI, BUFALINI CHAPEL.   Frescoes.
　　　　S. M. DEL POPOLO, IST CHAPEL, R.   Frescoes :
　　　　　　　Presepio.   Five lunettes with scenes from

---

* The fresco representing the last days of Moses, ascribed to Signorelli,
is by an unknown painter, who has many affinities with Pintoricchio, but
was more strongly influenced by Signorelli.

Rome (*Con.*),   the Life of St. Jerome. (These lunettes
in great part).

CHOIR. Ceiling frescoes, 1505.

San Gimigiano. MUNICIPIO. Madonna in Glory.

San Severino. DUOMO, SACRISTY. Madonna and Donor.

Siena.   SALA XI, 45. Holy Family.

DUOMO, LIBRERIA. Frescoes ; Life of Pius II.,
1503–1508.

LUNETTE OVER ENTRANCE. Fresco : Coronation of Pius III.

CAPPELLA DI S. GIOVANNI. Frescoes : Birth
of John ; Portraits of Alberto Aringhieri.
Paid for, 1504.

Spello.   COLLEGIATA, 2ND ALTAR R. Madonna.

BAGLIONI CHAPEL. Frescoes : Annunciation ;
Adoration of Magi ; Christ among the Doctors, 1501.

SACRISTY. Madonna, 1501.

OLD SACRISTY. Fresco : Angel.

S. ANDREA, R. TRANSEPT. Madonna and
Saints, 1508.

S. GIROLAMO, CLOISTER CHAPEL. Fresco :
Nativity. (?) E.

Spoleto.   DUOMO, 1ST CHAPEL R. Ruined Frescoes :
Madonna and Saints ; God and Angels ;
Dead Christ·

RAPHAEL.

1483–1520. Pupil of Timoteo Viti of Urbino ; assistant of
Perugino and Pintoricchio ; influenced by Leonardo,
Fra Bartolommeo, Michelangelo, and Sebastiano del
Piombo.

(See also Giulio Romano and Pierin del Vaga)

Bergamo. Lochis, 207. Bust of St. Sebastian. E.

Berlin. 141. Madonna. E.

145. Madonna and Saints, 1502.

247ᴬ. " Terranuova Madonna." E.

248. " Colonna Madonna" (in great part). E.

Bologna. St. Cecilia and other Saints (in great part).

Brescia. Gal. Tosio, Sala XIII, 37. Salvator Mundi.
E.

Buda-Pesth. 71. " Esterhazy Madonna." E.

72. Portrait of Young Man (completely repainted).

Chantilly. Musée Condé. Three Graces. E.
" Madonne d' Orléans." E.

Dresden. 93. " Sistine Madonna."

Florence. Pitti. 40. Leo X with Cardinals Giulio dei
Medici and L. dei Rossi, 1518.

59. Maddalena Doni. E.

61. Angelo Doni. E.

79. Portrait of Pope Julius II.

151. " Madonna della Sedia."

165. " Madonna del Baldacchino " (in very
small part).

174. Vision of Ezechiel (execution by Giulio
Romano).

178. " Granduca Madonna." E.

229. " La Donna Gravida." E.

245. " La Donna Velata."

Uffizi, 288. Portrait of Himself. E.

1139. " Madonna del Cardellino." E.

London. 168. St. Catherine.

213. The Knight's Vision. E.

1171. " Madonna Ansidei," 1506.

South Kensington. Cartoons for Tapestries
(execution not Raphael's, but chiefly by G.
F. Penni).

Mr. L. Mond. Crucifixion. E.

Madrid.	364. " Madonna dell'Agnello," 1507.
	365. " Madonna del Pesce," (execution chiefly by Giulio Romano).
	267. Portrait of Young Cardinal.
Milan.	BRERA, 270. Sposalizio, 1504.
Munich.	1049. " Madonna Cangiani " (in great part).
	1050. " Madonna Tempi." E.
Panshanger.	LORD COWPER. Madonna, 1508.
	Madonna. E.
Paris.	1496. " La Belle Jardinière," 1507–1508.
	1502. St. Michael. E.
	1503. St. George. E.
	1505. Portrait of Baldassare Castiglione, 1515.
	1498. " Sainte Famille de François I." (execution by Giulio Romano), 1518.
	1504. St. Michael crushing Satan (execution by Giulio Romano), 1518.
Perugia.	S. SEVERO. Fresco : Christ and Saints, 1505.
Rome.	BORGHESE, 369. Entombment, 1507.
	397. Portrait of Perugino. E.
	DORIA, 130. Portraits of Navagero and Beazzano.
	ACADEMY OF S. LUCA. Fresco : Putto with Garland.
	VATICAN GALLERY. Coronation and predelle : Adoration of Magi ; Presentation. E. The nine Virtues (monochrome), 1507. " Madonna di Foligno," with Sigismondo Conti as Donor. Transfiguration (upper part), 1519.
	STANZA DELLA SEGNATURA. Frescoes : CEILING : Allegorical figures of Theology, Philosophy, Poetry, and Jurisprudence : Fall of Man ; Judgment of Solomon ; Apollo and Marsyas ; an Angel surveying the Earth.

Rome (*Con.*). WALLS : The " Disputa "—Discussion concerning the Sacrament ; The School of Athens ; Parnassus ; Justice ; Julius II. and his Cardinals ; Justinian publishing the Pandects. All 1509–1511.

STANZA DELL' ELIODORO. Frescoes ; Heliodorus driven out of Temple (Pope Julius and his bearers executed by Raphael himself, the rest largely by assistants), 1511–1512. Miracle of Bolsena (the group of women L. not executed by Raphael). Finished Nov. 1, 1512. Attila turned away from Rome (the heads of Leo X. and his Cardinals in part from Raphael's own hand, the rest by pupils), 1514. Liberation of St. Peter (the entire execution by pupils, chiefly Giulio Romano), 1514.

STANZA DELL' INCENDIO DI BORGO. Frescoes : Fire in the environs of St. Peter's (execution almost wholly by Giulio Romano) ; Battle of Ostia (execution not Raphael's, chiefly Giulio Romano's).

LOGGIE. Fresco and stucco decorations : Illustrations to the Old Testament (their present condition is such that little can be said of the execution, save that it could not have been Raphael's. Some of the best seem to have been painted by P. del Vaga).

FARNESINA. Frescoes : Galatea, 1514.

Story of Cupid and Psyche (execution not by Raphael ; figures by Giulio Romano), 1517.

S. AGOSTINO. Fresco : the Prophet Isaiah.

S. M. DELLA PACE. Frescoes : Sibyls and Angels (in great part).

Vienna. 20. " Madonna im Grünen," 1506.

Volterra. PALAZZO INGHIRAMI. Portrait of Tommaso Inghirami (who died Sept. 5, 1516).

ROMANO *see* GIULIO.

SANO DI PIETRO.

Sienese.   1406–1481.   Pupil of Taddeo di Bartoli.

Altenburg.   Madonna with SS. Bernardino and Jerome and
        two Angels.
        Predelle : Visitation ; Assumption.
Barnard Castle.   Bowes Museum.   356.   Predella : Ex-
        orcism of Devil.
Bayeux.   32ᴬ.   Madonna, Christ and Angels.
Buda-Pesth.   23. Salome.
        32. A Monk.
        39. St. Bernardino.
Buonconvento.   SS. Pietro e Paolo, Sacristy.   Triptych :
        Madonna with SS. Catherine and Bernardino.
Chantilly.   Musée Condé, St. Francis and the three Virtues.
Dresden.   24. Parts of Polyptych.
        25. Painted Crucifix.
        26. Crucifixion.
Florence.   Sig. Bardini.   Madonna enthroned.
London.   Mr. C. Butler.   Sposalizio.
        Madonna with St. Antony Abbot and a Bishop.
Milan.   Prince Trivulzio.   Birth of Virgin.
Modena.   457. Nativity.   E.
New Haven, U. S. A.   Jarves Collection.   Coronation.
Oxford.   Christ Church.   15. Madonna and Saints.
        Taylorian, 14. Madonna.
Paris.   1128–1132.   Story of St. Jerome.
Pienza.   Duomo, L. Transept.   Madonna and four
        Saints.
Rome.   Vatican, Museo Cristiano, Case G, II. Na-
        tivity.
        III. Flight into Egypt.

Rome (*Con.*).   CASE N, VI. Presentation of Virgin.

      VII. Sposalizio.

      VIII. Madonna appearing to St. Dominic.

      IX, X, XII, XIII. Legends of Saints.

     CASE O. Three Women Praying and Three Spinning.

     CASE R, X. Nativity.

     CASE K. VIII. Nativity.

San Quirico di Val d'Orcia. COLLEGIATA. Polyptych.

Scotland.   GOSFORD HOUSE, LORD WEMYS. Large Cassone picture.

Siena.   SALA IV. All the pictures, 30 in number. (No. 10 dated 1447 ; No. 20, 1455–1458 ; No. 25, 1444).

    SALA V. All the pictures, 19 in number. (No. 2 dated 1460 ; No. 4, 1449 ; Nos. 8, 9, 1479).

    SALA VI.   1. Saints.

    2. Madonna and Saints.

    SALA VII, 25.   Madonna and Angels.

    ARCHIVIO. Book covers: Two Saints with Dove and Garland, 1457.

    God sending forth Angel of Wisdom, 1470.

    Marriage of Count Robert of Turin and the Daughter of Malavolti, 1472.

    Book. Statuto dell' Arte de Mercanzia : Miniature, 1472.

    PALAZZO PUBBLICO, GROUND FLOOR. Frescoes : Coronation, 1445 (in great part).   (In Spandril to R.) St. Bernardino.

    CORTE D'ASSISE. Fresco : St. Bernardino, 1460.

    PALAZZO PALMIERI-NUTI. Madonna and Saints.

    Cassoni : Story of Queen of Sheba ; Story of two Knights.

    CONFRATERNITÀ DELLA MADONNA SOTTO LE VOLTE DELL' OSPEDALE. Madonna.

Siena *(Con.).* DUOMO, LIBRERIA, Miniatures.

      S. GIROLAMO, SACRISTY. Coronation with St. Jerome and other Saints, 1465.

      ORATORIO DI S. BERNARDINO, UPPER CHAPEL. Madonna.

      OSSERVANZA, 1ST ALTAR, L. Madonna and Angels.

        3D ALTAR, L. Triptych.

        4TH ALTAR, L. Predella: Dead Christ and Saints.

      S. PIETRO ALLE SCALE, SACRISTY. Two small tondi: Gabriel and St. Lucy.

      PORTA ROMANA. Fresco: Coronation and Angels, 1459 (begun by Sassetta).

      RICOVERO (CAMPANSI), 1ST FLOOR. Fresco: Annunciation.

      CONFRATERNITÀ DELLA SS. TRINITÀ. Madonna with SS. Bernardino, Antony Abbot, and Angels.

Vienna. COUNT LANCKORONSKI. Bust of St. Francis. Two miracles of St. Bernardino.

SAN SEVERINO *see* LORENZO.

GIOVANNI SANTI.

1430/40-1494. Pupil of Melozzo da Forlì.

Berlin. 139. Madonna and Saints.

Cagli. S. DOMENICO, 1ST ALTAR, L. Frescoes: Madonna and Saints; Resurrection. EMBRASURE OF ARCH, Christ blessing and *putti.*

      R. WALL. Fresco: Christ with SS. Francis and Jerome.

Fano. SANTA CROCE, HIGH ALTAR. Madonna and Saints.

      S. M. NUOVA, 1ST ALTAR, L. Visitation.

Gradara (near Pesaro). MUNICIPIO. Madonna and Saints,
        1484.

London.   751. Madonna.

Milan.   BRERA, 188. Annunciation.

Montefiorentino. 1ST CHAPEL, R. Madonna, Saints, and
        Donor, 1489.

Rome.   LATERAN, 64. St. Jerome enthroned.

Scotland. LANGTON (NEAR DUNS), MRS. BAILLIE-HAMIL-
        TON. Profile Bust of a Boy.

Urbino.   2. Madonna with Saints, and the Buffi Family,
            1489.
        3. Dead Christ.
        4. Bust of Dead Christ with His Mother.
        5. Female Martyr.
        40. St. Roch. L.
        41. Tobias and the Angel. L.
        CASA DI RAFFAELE. Fresco : Madonna. (Ru-
            ined).
        S. SEBASTIANO, HIGH ALTAR. Martyrdom of
            St. Sebastian.

LUCA SIGNORELLI.

1441–1523. Pupil of Pier dei Franceschi ; influenced by An-
        tonio Pollaiuolo.

Altenburg. Nine sections of Polyptych.

Arcevia.   S. MEDARDO, CHOIR. Polyptych, 1507.
        Baptism (in part).

Arezzo.   MUSEO. David, Saints, and Prophets, 1519.
        DUOMO, SACRISTY. Three predelle.

Bergamo.   MORELLI, 19. St. Roch.
        20. Madonna.
        24. St. Sebastian.

Berlin.   79. Altar wings with three Saints each, 1498.
        79ᴬ. Pan. E.
        79ᴮ. Visitation.
        Portrait of Man. E.

Borgo Sansepolcro. MUNICIPIO. Standard : Deposition ;
    SS. Antonio and Egidio.

Castiglione Fiorentino. CAPPELLA DEL SACRAMENTO.
    Deposition (fresco).

Città di Castello. 17. Martyrdom of St. Sebastian, 1496.
        33. SS. Jerome, Margaret, Bernardino, Lucy,
        Michael, and the Baptist.
    PALAZZO MANCINI. Altar-piece : Madonna and
        Saints, 1515.
    Predella : Annunciation.
    PALAZZO PACI. Two predelle : Story of S.
        Cecilia.

Cortona. DUOMO. Conception (in very small part).
    Pietà and predelle, 1502.
    Communion of the Apostles, 1512.
    Incredulity of Thomas (?).
    Assumption (in small part).
    S. DOMENICO. Madonna and Saints, 1515.
    GESÙ. Madonna and four Saints. L.
    S. NICCOLÒ, HIGH ALTAR. Madonna and
        Saints ; Christ in Tomb. On the back of
        panel, Madonna and Saints. L.
    L. WALL. Ruined fresco. L.

Florence. ACADEMY, 164. Madonna and Saints, with pre-
        della. L.
    PITTI, 335. Holy Family. E.
    UFFIZI, 74. Madonna. E.
        1291. Holy Family. E.
        1298. Predella : Annunciation ; Adoration
        of Shepherds ; Adoration of Magi.
    CORSINI. Madonna and two Saints.

Foiano. COLLEGIATA. Coronation of Virgin, with St.
    Martin, 1523.

Liverpool. 25. Madonna (?).

London. 1128. Circumcision (the child completely re-
    painted by Sodoma). E.

London (*Con.*). MR. R. BENSON. Madonna. L.
　　　　　　Predelle : Pilgrims to Emaus ; Christ at
　　　　　　Emaus.
　　　　　LORD CRAWFORD. Two Predelle : Meeting of
　　　　　　Zacchariah and Elizabeth ; Birth of John.
　　　　　MR. L. MOND. Three Predelle.
　　　　　MR. MUIR MACKENZIE. Madonna (tondo).
Loreto.　SANTA CASA, L. SACRISTY. Frescoes : Christ
　　　　　　and the Apostles ; Conversion of Paul ;
　　　　　　Angels (in vault). E.
　　　　　CEILING OF NAVE. Medallion frescoes of
　　　　　　Prophets. E.
Meiningen. DUCAL PALACE. Small predelle.
Milan.　BRERA, 197 bis. Madonna and Saints, 1508.
　　　　　262. Flagellation. E.
　　　　　281. Madonna. E.
Monte Oliveto Maggiore. CLOISTER, Frescoes : Life of
　　　　　　St. Benedict, 1497.
Morra.　S. CRESCENZIANO. Frescoes : Flagellation; Cru-
　　　　　　cifixion. L.
Munich.　Madonna in Landscape.
New Haven, U. S. A. JARVES COLLECTION. Adoration
　　　　　　of Magi.
Orvieto.　OPERA DEL DUOMO. Fresco : Portraits of Sig-
　　　　　　norelli and Niccolò Vitelli. 1503.
　　　　　Mary Magdalen (in small part). 1504.
　　　　　DUOMO, CHAPEL R. TRANSEPT. Frescoes :
　　　　　　Last Judgment ; Anti-Christ ; Angels ;
　　　　　　Prophets ; Pietà ; Small Scenes and Deco-
　　　　　　rations. 1500–1504.
　　　　　The Prophets in vaulting, 1499.
Paris.　1525. Birth of Virgin. E.
　　　　　1527. Seven Heads (?).
Perugia.　DUOMO, WINTER CHAPEL. Madonna and Saints,
　　　　　　1484.
Richmond. SIR F. COOK. Two panels with fragments of
　　　　　　Baptism. E.

Richmond (*Con.*). Profile of Old Man.
Rome.   Rospigliosi, 3.   Madonna.
Scotland.   Pollock House (Pollockshaws).   Sir John
            Stirling-Maxwell. Predella : Pietà.   E.
Umbertide. S. Croce. Descent from Cross, and predella,
            1516.
Urbino.   S. Spirito.   Crucifixion, 1494.
            Pentecost, 1494.
Volterra.   Municipio.   Madonna and Saints, 1491.
            Duomo, Chapel of S. Carlo. Annunciation,
            1491.

SIMONE MARTINI.

Sienese.   1285(?)–1344. Pupil of Duccio ; slightly influenced
    by Giotto.

Antwerp.   257, 258. Annunciation.   L.
            259. Crucifixion.   L.
            260. Descent from Cross.   L.
Assisi.   S. Francesco, Lower Church, R. Transept.
            Fresco : SS. Francis, Louis of Toulouse,
            Clare, and another female Saint.
            Chapel of St. Martin. Frescoes : Legend
            of St. Martin and single figures of Saints.
Avignon.   Papal Palace, Salle de Consistoire. Frag-
            ments of frescoes : figures of Prophets and
            Sibyls.   After 1339.
            Chapelle de St. Jean. Frescoes : Life of
            John.   After 1339.
            Another Chapel. Frescoes : Legends of
            St. Marcel and other Saints. After 1339.
            Cathedral, Porch. Frescoes : Salvator
            Mundi ; Madonna and Angels.   After
            1339.

Florence.   UFFIZI, 23.   Annunciation and Saints* (assisted
by Lippo Memmi).   1333.

Liverpool.   8. Christ returning from the Doctors to His
Parents, 1342.

Naples.   S. LORENZO.   St. Louis of Toulouse crowning
his brother, Robert of Naples.   Also predelle.

Orvieto.   OPERA DEL DUOMO.   Polyptych, 1320.

Paris.   1383. Way to Golgotha.   L.

Pisa.   SALA III, 16–23.   Saints (originally part of
polyptych now in Seminario), 1320.

SEMINARIO, LIBRARY.   Polyptych, 1320.

Rome.   VATICAN, MUSEO CRISTIANO, CASE B, III.
Christ blessing.

Siena.   PALAZZO PUBBLICO, CORTE D' ASSISE.   Fresco:
Portrait of Guidoriccio da Fogliano on
Horseback, 1328.

Fresco: Madonna and Saints, 1315–1321.

S. AGOSTINO, CHOIR.   Triptych: Legend of
Beato Agostino Novello.   L.

LO SPAGNA.

Umbrian.   Active, 1500–1528.   Pupil of Perugino and Pintoricchio; influenced by Raphael.

Ashridge.   LORD BROWNLOW.   Female Saint.   E.

Assisi.   S. M. DEGLI ANGELI, CHAPEL OF S. BONAVEN-
TURA.   Frescoes: Saints.

S. FRANCESCO, LOWER CHURCH.   Madonna and
Saints, 1516.

Berlin.   MAGAZINE.   "Ancajani" Nativity.   E.

Caen.   3. Sposalizio.   E.
4. St. Jerome.   E.

* A charming imitation of this work, by an unknown hand,
is to be found in S. Pietro Ovile, at Siena.

Cambridge. U. S. A. MR. DENMAN ROSS. Bust of St. Sebastian. E. (Copy of Bergamo Raphael).

Florence. PITTI, 451bis. Madonna and Saints.

London. 1032. Agony in Garden.

HERTFORD HOUSE. St. Mary in Egypt.

MR. MOND. Three small panels: SS. Bernardino, Louis, and Magdalen.

Mells Park (Frome). MRS. JOHN HORNER. A kneeling Saint (fresco).

Milan. POLDI-PEZZOLI, 150. Madonna and two Angels.

Paris. 1539. Nativity. E.

1540. Madonna.

1568–70. Story of St. Jerome.

Perugia. SALA XI, 7. Madonna and Saints. E.

9. Beata Colomba (?).

SALA XII, 24. St. Clare.

25. St. Louis of Toulouse.

SALA XIII, 26. Fresco: St. Francis receiving Stigmata.

Rome. CAPITOL. Frescoes: The nine Muses.

COLONNA, 112. St. Jerome.

VATICAN GALLERY. Nativity. E.

Spoleto. MUNICIPIO. Frescoes: Madonna and four Saints. L.

Madonna with SS. Stephen and a Bishop. L. Two putti.

The Virtues (around a monument).

DUOMO, WINTER CHAPEL. Madonna and Saints.

S. GIACOMO (near Spoleto). Frescoes in Choir, 1526.

Todi. MUNICIPIO. Coronation and Saints, 1511.

Trevi. MUNICIPIO, 63. St. Catherine.

66. St. Cecilia.

Coronation with two predelle.

S. M. DELLE LAGRIME, CHAPEL L. TRANSEPT. Frescoes: Bishop enthroned; Entombment; Saints; Prophets. L.

Trevi (*Con.*). S. MARTINO, OUTSIDE CHAPEL.   Fresco : Madonna appearing to four Saints, 1511.
ALTAR L. Fresco : St. Martin and the Beggar.

TADDEO DI BARTOLI.

Sienese. About 1362–1422.   Pupil of Bartolo di Fredi.

Asciano.   COLLEGIATA.   Madonna.
Florence.   PALAZZO PANCIATICHI.   St. Elizabeth of Hun-
gary.
Montepulciano.   DUOMO.   Reredos, 1400.
Münster in W.   KUNSTVEREIN, 1149.   Assassination of
Peter Martyr.
Naples.   SALA DEI BIZANTINI, 10.   Small St. Sebastian.
DUOMO, CHAPEL TO R. OF CHOIR.   Triptych :
Madonna and Saints.
Oldenburg.   24.   St. Mark.
25.   St. John.
26.   St. Luke.
27.   St. Matthew.
Paris.   1152.   St. Peter.
Madonna and four Saints, 1490.
Pisa.   MUSEO CIVICO, SALA V, 22. S. Donino ; on
back, Crucifixion.
FORMER SACRISTY OF S. FRANCESCO.   Frescoes : Apostles visiting Virgin ; Death of
Virgin ; Mourning over her Body ; Funeral ;
and single Figures.   1397.
Perugia.   SALA IV, 5.   Polyptych : St. Francis, Antony
of Padua, Louis and other Saints.
6.   St. Paul.
7.   St. Peter.
9.   Polyptych : Madonna and Saints.
10.   Pentecost, 1403.
15.   Madonna (from an Annunciation).

Rome.   VATICAN, MUSEO CRISTIANO, CASE F, XIII.
Small Triptych : Crucifixion and Saints.
CASE K, V. Assumption of Virgin.

S. Gimigiano. MUNICIPIO. Polyptych : Madonna, Christopher, Nicholas of Bari, and other Saints.
S. Gimigiano, and Scenes from his Life.

COLLEGIATA. Frescoes : Heaven, Hell, Saints, and Annunciation, 1403.

Siena.   SALA II, 72. Adoration of Magi.
73. Triptych.
74. St. Peter Martyr.
75. St. Agnes.
76. Annunciation, 1409.
77. Nativity.
78. Triptych.
79. Martyrdom of SS. Cosmas and Damian.
80. St. Matthew.
88, 89. Annunciation.

PALAZZO PUBBLICO, CHAPEL. Frescoes : Death of Virgin, 1407.

ANTECHAPEL. Allegorical Frescoes. Finished, 1414.

OPERA DEL DUOMO. Paintings to illustrate the Creed.

ABBAZIA DI S. EUGENIO, SACRISTY. St. Ansano and a Bishop.

COMPAGNIA DI S. CATERINA SOTTO SPEDALE. Triptych. 1400.

S. FRANCESCO, R. WALL. Visitation (ruined fresco).

OSSERVANZA, 4TH ALTAR, L. Polyptych. 1413.

SERVI, 4TH ALTAR, R. (above altar-piece by Matteo). Nativity, 1404.

SPEDALE, INFERMERIA DI S. GALGANO. Fresco : Crucifixion.

INFERMERIA DELLE DONNE. Crucifixion (panel).

Volterra.   DUOMO. CHAPEL OF S. CARLO. Triptych:
Madonna and Saints, 1411.

PIERINO DEL VAGA.*

1501–1547.   Pupil perhaps of Ridolfo Ghirlandaio, or Fra
Bartolommeo, and certainly of Raphael; influenced
by Michelangelo.
(See also Raphael.)

Florence.   COUNT RODONI. Version of "Loreto Madonna."

Genoa.   PALAZZO DORIA. Fragments of frescoes.

London.   LORD NORTHBROOK. Holy Family (mono-
chrome).
Madonna.
MARQUIS OF NORTHAMPTON. Madonna.

Narbonne.   Fresco from the Villa Magliana : Martyrdom of
St. Cecilia (lunette).

Pisa.   S. MATTEO, L. WALL. Triptych : Holy Family
with warrior Saint and Bishop. L.

Richmond.   SIR F. COOK. Altar-piece : Nativity, 1533.

Rome.   BORGHESE, 358. Nativity.
VATICAN, STANZA DELLA SEGNATURA. Small
frescoes in monochrome under Raphael's
paintings.
STANZA DELL 'ELIODORO. Monochrome frescoes under Raphael's paintings. E.
BORGIA APARTMENT, ANTECHAMBER. Ceiling
frescoes.
LOGGIE. Abraham and the Angels. Jacob
and Rachel. Joseph and his Brothers.
Joseph and Pharaoh's Dream. Israelites
crossing Red Sea. Moses on Sinai ; probably many others. All E.

Vienna.   PRINCE LICHTENSTEIN, 24. Holy Family.

* More important works only.

LORENZO VECCHIETTA.

Sienese. Circa 1412–1480. Architect, Sculptor, and Painter.
Pupil of Taddeo di Bartoli.

Buda-Pesth. 21. St. Luke.

Florence. UFFIZI, 47. Madonna and Saints, 1457.

Pienza. DUOMO, CHAPEL L. OF CHOIR. Triptych:
Assumption of Virgin, 1461.

Siena. SALA III, 63. St. Bernardino.
67. Madonna and four Saints, 1477.
SALA X, 5. Cartoon for Tabernacle now in
Cathedral, 1465.
ARCHIVIO. Book covers: Madonna crowning
Pius II, 1460.
Angels holding Screen, 1458.
PALAZZO PUBBLICO, UFFICIO STATO CIVILE
(GROUND FLOOR). Fresco: Madonna of
Mercy, 1461.
UPPER ROOM. Preaching of St. Bernardino.
Miracle of the Saint's dead Body.
PALAZZO PALMIERI–NUTI. Cassone: Battle
and Reconciliation.
PALAZZO SARACINI. Madonna and two Angels.
St. Martin and the Beggar.
BAPTISTERY. Frescoes in vaulting and apse,
and on wall L. (from spectator) of apse.
1450–1453.
S. BARTOLOMMEO (CONTRADA DELL' ISTRICE),
SACRISTY. Madonna and five Angels.
SPEDALE, INFERMERIA DI S. PIETRO. All the
frescoes on walls and ceilings. 1448.
PELLEGRINAIO. Fresco 1st on L. 1441.
CHURCH, SACRISTY. Paintings on Shrine.
1445.

VITERBO *see* LORENZO.

FRANCESCO ZAGANELLI* (Da Cotignola).

Active chiefly first 30 years of XVI century.   Pupil of Pal-
    mezzano ;   influenced by Ercole Roberti and Rondi-
    nelli.

Aix (en Provence).   84. Madonna and Angels.
Bergamo.   MORELLI, 15. St. Antony preaching to the
        Fishes.
Berlin.   236, 241. Miracles of St. Antony of Padua.
        1164. Annunciation.
        HERR WESENDONCK, 2. Madonna.
Béziers.   224. St. Francis.
Faenza.   Dead Christ and Saints, with View of Faenza
        below.
Ferrara.   SALA IV. St. Sebastian, 1513.
Forlì.   Mystic Conception, 1513.
Lille.   Lunette : Pietà.
London.   THE MISSES COHEN. SS. Blaise, Roch, and
        another Saint (?).
        SIR W. CONWAY. St. Catherine.
        MR. H. REGINALD CORBETT. SS. Catherine
        and Francis reading.
        MR. MUIR MACKENZIE. Annunciation.
Milan.   BRERA. 196. Madonna and Saints (assisted by
        Bernardino Zaganelli), 1504.
        203. Madonna and Saints, 1505.
        BORROMMEO. St. Jerome.
        CASA SORMANI. Nativity.
Münster i/W. 46. St. Antony Abbot.
Naples.   SALA DEI CARACCI, 4. Sposalizio.
Ravenna.   306. Profile Portrait of Young Man.
        315. Baptism.
        330. Madonna.
        Large Altar-piece : Crucifixion.
        Two panels : St. Catherine ; St. Sebastian.

        * More tolerable works only.

Richmond. SIR F. COOK. St. Bernardino.
St. Francis.
St. Antony of Padua.
St. Catherine.
Rimini. MUNICIPIO. SS. Sebastian, Lawrence, and Jerome.
Rome. DON MARCELLO MASSARENTI. Holy Family.
Scotland. LINLATHEN, COL. ERSKINE. Baptism, with Dead Christ and Angels in lunette.
NEW BATTLE, MARQUIS OF LOTHIAN. Crucifixion.
Strassburg. Madonna and St. Catherine.

INDEX OF PLACES.

Buda-Pesth. GALLERY : Balducci, Benvenuto di Giovanni, Bertucci, Fungai, Giulio Romano, Lippo Memmi, Pietro Lorenzetti, Niccolò da Foligno, Pacchia, Pintoricchio, Raphael, Sano di Pietro, Vecchietta.

Bulciago. CHURCH : Palmezzano.

Buonconvento. Ss. PIETRO E PAOLO : Matteo di Giovanni, Pacchiarotto, Sano di Pietro.

Caen. MUSÉE : Lo Spagna.

Cagli. S. DOMENICO : Giovanni Santi.

Cambridge U. S. A. MR. DENMAN ROSS : Lo Spagna.

Casate Nuovo. CHURCH : Palmezzano.

Castiglione Fiorentino. CAPPELLA DEL SACRAMENTO : Signorelli.

Chalons sur Marne. MUSÉE : Bernardino di Mariotto.

Chantilly. MUSÉE CONDÉ : Sano di Pietro, Raphael.

Chiusi. DUOMO : Fungai, Peruzzi.

Cologne. GALLERY : Balducci, Gianniccolo Manni, Lippo Memmi.

Cortona. S. DOMENICO : Signorelli.
DUOMO : Pietro Lorenzetti, Signorelli.
GESÙ : Signorelli.
S. MARCO : Pietro Lorenzetti.
S. NICCOLÒ : Signorelli.

Cremona. S. AGOSTINO : Perugino.

Dijon. MUSÉE : Palmezzano.

Diruta. SIGNORA G. C. MORGANTI : Niccolò da Foligno.
S. ANTONIO : Fiorenzo di Lorenzo.
S. FRANCESCO : Eusebio di San Giorgio.

Dresden. GALLERY : Balducci, Genga, Giulio Romano, Peruzzi, Pintoricchio, Raphael, Sano di Pietro.

Empoli. OPERA DEL DUOMO : Bonfigli.

Faenza. MUSEO : Bertucci, Palmezzano, Francesco Zaganelli.
SIGNOR VINCENZO GUIDI : Bertucci.

13

Fano. S. Agostino : Perugino.
SANTA CROCE : Giovanni Santi.
S. MARIA NUOVA : Perugino, Giovanni Santi.

Ferrara. PINACOTECA : Francesco Zaganelli.

Florence. ACADEMY : Gentile da Fabriano, Ambrogio
Lorenzetti, Pietro Lorenzetti, Pacchiarotto,
Perugino, Signorelli.

PITTI : Beccafumi, Fiorenzo di Lorenzo, Genga,
Perugino, Raphael, Signorelli, Lo Spagna.

UFFIZI : Beccafumi, Brescianino, Genga, Gentile da Fabriano, Pietro Lorenzetti, Neroccio di Landi, Palmezzano, Perugino, Pier
dei Franceschi, Raphael, Signorelli, Simone
Martini, Vecchietta.

VIA FAENZA, CENACOLO DI FOLIGNO : Perugino.

SIGNOR BARDINI : Benvenuto di Giovanni, Lippo
Memmi, Sano di Pietro.

CORSINI GALLERY : Signorelli.

MARCHESE IPPOLITO GINORI : Bertucci.

PALAZZO PANCIATICHI : Taddeo di Bartoli.

COUNT RODONI : Pierin del Vaga.

MARCHESE PIO STROZZI : B. di Giovanni.

PALAZZO TORRIGIANI : Beccafumi, Gianniccolo
Manni.

SS. ANNUNZIATA : Perugino.

LA CALZA : Perugino.

SANTA CROCE, REFECTORY : Brescianino.

S. M. MADDALENA DEI PAZZI : Perugino.

S. SPIRITO : Perugino.

Foiano. COLLEGIATA : Signorelli.

Foligno. SS. ANNUNZIATA : Perugino.
S. BARTOLOMMEO : Niccolò da Foligno.
S. MARIA IN CAMPIS : Niccolò da Foligno.
S. MARIA INFRA PORTIS : Niccolò da Foligno.
S. NICCOLÒ : Niccolò da Foligno.

Forlì.   PINACOTECA : Melozzo, Palmezzano, Francesco Zaganelli.

S. BIAGIO E GIROLAMO : Palmezzano.

S. MERCURIALE : Palmezzano.

Frankfort a/M.   STÄDL-INSTITUT : Boccatis, Fiorenzo di Lorenzo, Gianniccolo Manni, Neroccio di Landi, Perugino.

Genoa.   PALAZZO DORIA : Pierin del Vaga.

S. STEFANO : Giulio Romano.

Glasgow.   GALLERY : Brescianino.

Gradara (near Pesaro).   MUNICIPIO : Giovanni Santi.

Gualdo-Tadino.   PINACOTECA : Niccolò da Foligno.

DUOMO : Bernardino di Mariotto, Niccolò da Foligno.

Gubbio.   MUNICIPIO : Balducci.

Hamburg.   CONSUL WEBER : Beccafumi, Palmezzano.

Karlsruhe.   GALLERY : Niccolò da Foligno, Palmezzano.

Leipzig.   GALLERY : Pintoricchio.

Lille.   MUSÉE : Francesco Zaganelli.

Liverpool.   WALKER GALLERY : Benvenuto di Giovanni, Fungai, Palmezzano, Signorelli, Simone Martini.

London.   NATIONAL GALLERY : Beccafumi, Benvenuto di Giovanni, Bertucci, Duccio, Fungai, Genga, Giulio Romano, Ambrogio Lorenzetti, Lorenzo di San Severino the Younger, Gianniccolo Manni, Matteo di Giovanni, Niccolò da Foligno, Pacchia, Palmezzano, Perugino, Pier dei Franceschi, Pintoricchio, Raphael, Giovanni Santi, Signorelli, Lo Spagna.

SOUTH KENSINGTON MUSEUM : Raphael.

LORD ALDENHAM : Bertucci.

LORD ASHBURNHAM : Benvenuto di Giovanni.

MR. ROBERT BENSON : Beccafumi, Duccio, Signorelli.

London (*Con.*). Bridgewater House (Lord Ellesmere): Peruzzi.

 Mr. Charles Butler : Boccatis, Francesco di Giorgio, Matteo di Giovanni, Neroccio di Landi, Pacchiarotto, Sano di Pietro.

 The Misses Cohen : Francesco Zaganelli.

 Sir William Conway : Francesco Zaganelli.

 Mr. H. Reginald Corbett : Francesco Zaganelli.

 Lord Crawford : Balducci, Duccio, Signorelli.

 Dorchester House (Captain Holford): Perugino.

 Hertford House : Beccafumi, Lo Spagna.

 Sir H. Howarth : Genga.

 Mr. Muir Mackenzie : Pacchiarotto, Perugino, Signorelli.

 Mr. Ludwig Mond : Genga, Matteo di Giovanni, Peruzzi, Raphael, Signorelli, Lo Spagna.

 Lord Northampton : Pierin del Vaga.

 Lord Northbrook. Pierin del Vaga.

 Dr. J. P. Richter : Bernardino di Mariotto.

 Mr. George Salting : Benvenuto di Givanni.

 Mr. Henry Wagner : Bonfigli.

 Lord Wantage : Perugino.

Loreto. Santa Casa : Melozzo, Signorelli.

Lucca. Pinacoteca : Beccafumi.

Lyons. Musée : Perugino.

Madrid. Museo del Prado : Giulio Romano, Peruzzi, Raphael.

Mantua. Palazzo Gonzaga : Giulio Romano.

 Palazzo del Tè : Giulio Romano.

Marseilles. Musée : Perugino.

Matelica. S. Francesco : Eusebio di San Giorgio, Palmezzano.

INDEX OF PLACES 199

Perugia. PINACOTECA : Benvenuto di Giovanni, Boccatis,
Bonfigli, Domenico di Bartolo, Duccio,
Eusebio di San Giorgio, Fiorenzo di Lo-
renzo, Gentile da Fabriano, Gianniccolo
Manni, Bernardino di Mariotto, Niccolò da
Foligno, Perugino, Pier dei Franceschi,
Pintoricchio, Lo Spagna, Taddeo di Bartoli.

Perugia. CAMBIO : Gianniccolo Manni, Perugino.
MUNICIPIO : Fiorenzo di Lorenzo.
DUOMO : Fiorenzo di Lorenzo, Signorelli.
S. FIORENZO : Bonfigli.
S. PIETRO : Bonfigli, Eusebio di San Giorgio,
Gianniccolo Manni, Perugino.
S. SEVERO : Perugino, Raphael.

Pienza. DUOMO : Matteo di Giovanni, Sano di Pietro,
Vecchietta.

Pisa. MUSEO : Gentile da Fabriano, Simone Martini,
Taddeo di Bartoli.
CAMPO SANTO : Unknown Follower of the Lo-
renzetti.
DUOMO : Beccafumi.
S. MATTEO : Pierin del Vaga.
SEMINARIO : Simone Martini.

Ravenna. PINACOTECA : Palmezzano, Francesco Zaganelli.

Richmond. SIR FRANCIS COOK : Balducci, Benvenuto di
Giovanni, Francesco di Giorgio, Bernardino
di Mariotto, Signorelli, Pierin del Vaga,
Francesco Zaganelli.

Rimini. MUNICIPIO : Francesco Zaganelli.
S. FRANCESCO : Pier di Franceschi.

Rome. CASTLE OF SANT' ANGELO : Pintoricchio.
VILLA ALBANI : Niccolò da Foligno, Perugino,
Peruzzi.
BARBERINI : Giulio Romano.
BORGHESE : Giulio Romano, Peruzzi, Pintoric-
chio, Raphael, Pierin del Vaga.

Scotland (*Con.*). NEW BATTLE, MARQUIS OF LOTHIAN: Bertucci, Pacchia, Francesco Zaganelli.

POLLOCK HOUSE (Pollockshaws), SIR JOHN STIRLING-MAXWELL: Signorelli.

ROSSIE PRIORY, LORD KINNAIRD: Pacchiarotto.

Siena. PINACOTECA: Balducci, Beccafumi, Benvenuto di Giovanni, Brescianino, Domenico di Bartoli, Duccio, Francesco di Giorgio, Fungai, Genga, Ambrogio Lorenzetti, Pietro Lorenzetti, Matteo di Giovanni, Neroccio di Landi, Pacchia, Pacchiarotto, Peruzzi, Pintoricchio, Sano di Pietro, Taddeo di Bartoli, Vecchietta.

ARCHIVIO: Benvenuto di Giovanni, Francesco di Giorgio, Fungai, Ambrogio Lorenzetti, Neroccio di Landi, Sano di Pietro, Vecchietta.

ARCO DELLE DUE PORTE: Peruzzi.

OPERA DEL DUOMO: Balducci, Beccafumi, Duccio, Genga, Ambrogio Lorenzetti, Pietro Lorenzetti, Matteo di Giovanni, Taddeo di Bartoli.

PALAZZO PUBBLICO: Beccafumi, Ambrogio Lorenzetti, Sano di Pietro, Simone Martini, Taddeo di Bartoli, Vecchietta.

PORTA ROMANA: Sano di Pietro.

BELCARO (near Siena). Matteo di Giovanni, Peruzzi.

PALAZZO BINDI-SERGARDI: Beccafumi.

PALAZZO PALMIERI-NUTI: Benvenuto di Giovanni, Brescianino, Fungai, Matteo di Giovanni, Pacchia, Pacchiarotto, Sano di Pietro, Vecchietta.

PALAZZO POLLINI: Peruzzi.